Celebrating Compassion

The Liberating Spirituality of Forgiving

Gerard Martin

ISBN 978-1-0980-0666-2 (paperback)
ISBN 978-1-0980-0688-4 (hardcover)
ISBN 978-1-0980-0667-9 (digital)

Copyright © 2019 by Gerard Martin

All rights reserved. No part of this publication may be reproduced, distributed, or transmitted in any form or by any means, including photocopying, recording, or other electronic or mechanical methods without the prior written permission of the publisher. For permission requests, solicit the publisher via the address below.

Christian Faith Publishing, Inc.
832 Park Avenue
Meadville, PA 16335
www.christianfaithpublishing.com

Presuming the good will of those sighted in this work, all text and quotes have intentionally been adapted to use inclusive language, if indeed the quote still makes good sense.

Unless otherwise indicated, all the Scriptures are taken from The New Oxford Annotated Bible, Third Edition, New Revised Standard Version. Oxford University Press, 2001.

All quotations regarding Divine Mercy are taken verbatim and without alteration from the Diary of St. Maria Faustina Kowalska, *Marian Press, Stockbridge. MA 2008, and noted by number.*

Printed in the United States of America

To all who have compassionately forgiven me

my own trespasses in life,

and thereby,

taught me Christic love,

and hence,

the sanctifying significance of mercy.

Contents

Introduction 9

1. Operative Mercy 15
Scripture's *Amma* Mercy 18
Mercy's Amnesty 23
Satanic Tabulator 23
Mercy's Essential Conditions 25
Divine Amnesia 26
Mercy and Memory 28
Conscience and Guilt 28
God's Defining Feature 29

2. Christic Compassion 31
Jesus' "Set Up" Question 32
Jesus' Self-definition 33
Jesus: Healer and Forgiver 34
Compassion's Fuller Picture 36
Jesus' Penchant for Sinners 39

3. Abba Mercy 44
Mercy's Caressing 44
Mercy's verses Self-righteousness 45

Mercy's Symbols: Robe, Ring, and Sandals..........48

Mercy's Human Dignity...............................49

Mercy's Risk...51

Abba Mercy Resume 51

4. **The Why of Mercy** **53**

Two Vying Spirits......................................54

Historical Jesus and Mercy 56

Forgiving Mercy and Personal Peace................59

Mercy's Demonic Foe..................................60

Mercy and Justice......................................62

Mercy for the Love of Christ 64

A Time for Building Bridges 65

5. **How to Be Merciful?** **66**

Time Heals: If..68

Bonfire of Hurt...73

Mercy and Memory 75

Healing Prayer: A Blessing Prayer...................76

Self-forgiveness...79

6. **Rethinking "Unforgivable" Pain**........................ **82**

Life's Puzzle...83

The Paschal Piece......................................84

Rites of Passage Contribution 85

The School of Humility and Pain....................86

Descending into Pain..................................88

Emptying Self of Self 89

O Happy Fault..92

Ascending from Pain..................................93

7. **Parameters of Divine Mercy**........................ **96**
   Unqualified Divine Mercy 96
   Creature "I" and Divine Mercy 98
   Divine Mercy's Compatibility 101
   Divine Mercy and Lingering Crosses...............106
   Dark Nights' Revelation..............................110
   Spirituality's Masquerade.............................113

8. **Sacraments of Mercy**............................... **115**
   Baptism's Compassion.................................116
   Eucharist's Reconciliation............................117
   Sacramental Reconciliation 121
   Reconciliation: All Jesus' Idea.......................123
   Anointing's Reconciliation 126
   Holy Orders and Mercy 131

9. **Mercy's Summation** **133**

Introduction

There are two conspicuous clusters of flowers on the burning bush of divine mercy. One cluster blooms in celebration of an "as long as you did it to me" (Mt 25:31f) form of mercy. It rises out of empathy and solidarity with our less fortunate sisters and brothers who lack honest justice and peace. It addresses their human needs, e.g., health, poverty, natural disasters, and malnutrition. Because they directly focus more on human bodily needs, these blossoms are traditionally referred to as "the corporal works of mercy."

The second group of blooms are the "the spiritual works of mercy." They are more about nourishing the human soul. They are concerned with advising and consoling others. They include the virtue of pardoning, as well as bearing wrongs patiently. This is a book about the spiritual work of mercy called "forgiving."

To help clarify our theme of forgiveness, it is worth noting that while all mercy is about compassion, not all compassion is about forgiving. The terms "mercy" and "forgiveness" may be taken as nouns. Consequently, the singular term "forgiving mercy" may appear to be redundant. However, besides being used as a verb, "forgiving" can also be used as an adjective. As such, it takes the generic term of "mercy" and modifies it. It indicates the caliber or type of mercy being exercised. Forgiving mercy is but one indispensable thread in the entire tapestry of mercy.

Knowing how to chemically define water or oxygen doesn't mean a person even begins to understand what either one really is. It's so easy for us to take either one for granted—until we can't get our breath—or are on the verge of severe dehydration and can't get water. Then and there, it's the blunt experience of needing, but lacking either one or both, which teaches, clarifies, and in a certain sense, defines the realities of water or oxygen. The same could be said of mercy! We might well be able to talk about, quote sacred scriptures or poets or instruct others as to how forgiving mercy works. However, scores of people have no effective idea of what mercy actually is, until they personally need and can't get any or find it so difficult to be merciful toward someone else—maybe even themselves! It's then that theory sheepishly fades in meaning.

Mercy needed, pardon given, are each potentially sage teachers of the true, inner meaning of forgiving mercy. Active forgiving is not realistically learned from books. At best, while books often inspire because they are filled with solid devotion and piety, they merely point us into a helpful direction. This is a book, not only for those who find it very difficult to forgive, but for those who yearn for forgiveness—but can't find any. Depending upon the weight of a personal offense, some people do really well in being forgivers. They try with all their heart to choose their own peace. This book is also for them.

While offering solid, spiritual groundwork for mercy, this book delves into the very practical modes of being

INTRODUCTION

compassionately forgiving. That may sound like a straight-forward, easy-to-understand theme. It is anything but. Why? Because the very words *mercy* and *forgiving* are often so emotionally packed, they convey strikingly diverse realities to so many different people.

First of all, for some people, forgiving another suggests a surrender, a personal failure of giving in to offenders. It's an unhealthy cop-out, an embarrassing weakness. They equate withholding mercy with a form of garnered strength, thereby, making clear their rejection of both an offense and the offender.

For others, the very suggestion of forgiving is a disarming distraction to what's going on in their life—and they don't want to be distracted! It's a vile intrusion into their righteous arena of justice. Even though in reality, mercy and justice are actually Siamese twins congenitally joined at the heart. To attempt a separation—or to place them in diametric opposition to each other—only causes irreparable, essential disfigurement to both.

Equally born of divine love, mercy actually perfects justice. "Only through mercy can justice be delivered... Where there is no mercy, there is no justice" (Pope Francis, March 23, 2015 homily). "God's justice is his mercy" (cf. Ps 51:11–16). "Mercy surpasses justice" (*Misericordiae Vultus,* Bull of Indiction of Extraordinary Jubilee of Mercy, n. 20 and 21).

There certainly are no easy, quick steps to mitigate deep, offensive hurt, but for the Christian, sharing in Jesus' mercy is integral to the process. Once a person truly loves, mercy flows naturally, though not necessarily easily. A person who puts tensions between love and mercy needs to

CELEBRATING COMPASSION

be blessed with someone to truly love and by whom to be loved and then learn from that experience. Choosing to forgive is to turn over one's insistent wounds into God's loving and healing hands.

There are some people who can love only perfect people. That's the challenging rub! Forgiving is precisely about loving imperfect people. "If you love only those who love you—even tax collectors do that" (Mt 5:46). "But I say to you who listen, love your enemies, do good to those who hate you, bless those who curse you, pray for those who abuse you... Be merciful, just as your Father is merciful" (Lk 6:27, 36). Pope Francis prods: "If you can't forgive, ask for more faith" (November 10, 2014, Homily, Casa Santa Marta); on a later occasion: "If you can't forgive, you are not a Christian" (Homily, Santa Marta, September 9, 2015). Forgiving mercy addresses sin and imperfect people directly. That's why honest, forgiving mercy does not always come easy. "But with God all things are possible" (Mk 10:27).

Some forgiveness, due to the depth of the offense, is often a lonely, solitary decision. By nature, it demands considerable inner work and reflection. There has to be the desire and willpower not to carry the baggage of unforgiveness to the grave. Of course, that's my choice. If I choose to, I certainly can do exactly that. Choosing otherwise, however, the journey of forgiving has to be very intentionally decided with sincere and unwavering resolve. Otherwise, we commit ourselves to live trapped in the cage of the past. Again, that's our choice. The merciful person has to be able to envision light beyond the darkness, health beyond the

INTRODUCTION

sickness, joy beyond the pain, love beyond the sin—just as Jesus did.

In preference to feeding the urge to punish or to get even, mercy strives to tame and temper one's own restless heart. Further, mercy informs us: God doesn't need or appoint us (me) to make sure someone else pays for his/her sins. But at the end of the day, forgiving mercy has to do with holiness, i.e., a vulnerable sharing in divine mystery. We discover the path to being merciful only when we partake in that divine mystery. When God's essential holiness is found within us, it's called "Christlikeness."

Hence, forgiving becomes a ministry of compassionate healing. With Christic intention, it pauses to lift up a weak and wounded fellow pilgrim from the ditch of failure and remorse. It reaches in to pour on the healing oils of compassion. However, mercy is not only an outgoing ministry. There's always a resultant, remedial ministering to one's self.

Jesus as "the Christ" by name and title epitomizes love's mercy. It's his most outstanding revelation. As "the Christ," he bequeathed compassionate love to the Church as a prophecy, i.e., a truth not only to unequivocally proclaim but to effectively practice. In his *Apostolic Letter* at the conclusion of the *Extraordinary Jubilee of Mercy*, Pope Francis strongly agrees: "Mercy cannot become a mere parenthesis in the life of the Church, it constitutes her very existence" (*Misericordia et misera*, n. 1). Consequently, whoever has been baptized has already been anointed to also be courageously prophetical, i.e., to be a staunch mentor and witness to operative forgiving mercy.

CELEBRATING COMPASSION

Divine Mercy began in the Garden of Eden with an offended God promising to send a redeeming "beloved son" (Mk 9:7).

Forgiveness begins with a single person, with you, with me. Imagine if all of us who call ourselves "Christian" would genuinely and humbly forgive each other. What peace and freedom would be unleashed in a Spirit-enflamed, beatitudinal witness to the world! It could well transform it. "Blessed are the merciful, for they will receive mercy" (Mt 5:7). "Mankind will not have peace until it turns to the fount of My mercy" (Faustina Diary, n. 699). What a divine prediction!

Talk about *celebrating compassion*! Consequently, the more we know about *the liberating spirituality of forgiving*, the better.

1

Operative Mercy

Let's consider the title of this chapter. The word *operative* simply means "actively/actually working." This doesn't mean simply functioning, but whatever the effort or energy is, it's effective. In other words, there are results.

As mentioned in the *Introduction*, there are multiple purposes of mercy referred to as "corporal and spiritual works of mercy." Each and all center upon the human person, so there's a bleed-through, i.e., an overlap between them, a mutual energizing. This just indicates there are at least several ways to approach mercy in general. There are multiple reasons for this or that type of mercy. Just what is forgiving mercy in particular?

Often enough, people use the same word to describe what they believe is a commonly understood reality. But even though using the identical word, upon some discussion, they discover they don't mean the same thing at all. "Mercy" is one of those words. Why is that? Because taken generically, "mercy" can mean many different things. How does that happen? First of all, there's a very broad spectrum of mercy derived from responding to purely human needs and perspectives. Such approaches are often couched in rich, varied cultures and habits. Then there are religious overtones which affect and flavor a "generalized" mercy. "Forgiving mercy" is a very special form of compassion. Additionally, what particularizes forgiving even further is—depending upon its gravity—it often carries a lot of emotional baggage with it. So what is "forgiving mercy" from a solid Judeo-Christian perspective, i.e., before we get our human hands, minds, and a personal preferences around it?

As everyone knows from personal experience, forgiving is not always so simple or easy. Religious scholars inform us that compassion is found at the very heart of every major religion in the world. That's because forgiveness is a fairly universal need. Nobody gets through life without offending somebody; nobody gets through life without being offended. "Mercy," says Pope Francis, is "the fundamental law that dwells in the heart of every person who looks sincerely into the eyes of his brothers and sisters on the path of life" (*Misericordiae Vultus*, n. 2). As Christians, we believe Jesus of Nazareth is God's mercy made flesh. Hence, it makes sense to delve into the Judeo-Christian revelation regarding not only mercy in general but forgiving mercy in particular.

Bible students advise us there is not a sole, all-comprehensive word for mercy in the scriptures. Mercy is too rich a treasure. Rather, we've got to look at several terms for their nuanced, flavoring contribution to get a fuller, panoramic picture of forgiving mercy.

OPERATIVE MERCY

For instance, one Hebrew word for mercy is *hesed*. But unable to contain the full meaning of mercy in a single term or notion, *hesed* is surrounded by other descriptive word qualifiers. For instance, there's "faith, steadfastness, and loyalty," all having to do with trust and reliability. Surely, sincere forgiving involves a considerable measure of focused decision-making. But rather than being a predominantly punitive decision, *hesed* focuses on being a proactive deliverer. You may interject: "A what?"

Hesed tells us that to be truly merciful is to be much more than just a person who "let's people off the hook." To be a genuine, merciful person means to be a restorative person, i.e., a rehabilitating influence in the life of an offender. Undoubtedly, that's an immediate turnoff for some people. Nevertheless, it's key to Christian forgiveness. It pertains to mercy's very nature. In other words, no matter what it looks like, without these relevant qualities of being restorative and rehabilitating, the forgiving act lacks its inner power to holistically renew either the forgiver or the forgiven. So these inner "ingredients" shouldn't be shoved to the side just because we've got to rethink our attitudes, or it might be hard to accomplish. Why not? Because being "a proactive deliverer, a restorative person, a rehabilitating influence" is, at heart, God's own revelation to us regarding full-fledged divine mercy.

It's been noted that while the word *justice* appears 142 times in sacred scripture, *mercy* and its equivalents appear nearly twice as often. Evidently, this overwhelming emphasis is equally at the heart of God's revelation. In other words, it has divine purpose. God has reasons. Let's consider some more of these instructive words for mercy.

CELEBRATING COMPASSION

Scripture's *Amma* Mercy

There is *rahamin*, describing a feminine, derivative mercy. That's understandable because r*ehem* means "a womb." Hence, it's an *amma* mercy germinating within the soul of the mother concomitantly with her infant. It's not a mercy bequeathed out of obligation or responsibility but naturally derives from an inner love conviction welling up right from within the mothering. "Womb mercy" is factually a bone-of-my-bone, flesh-of-my-flesh mercy. As such, it has an irrevocable quality. This is all quite understandable since modern medicine reports that during human gestation, there's an actual, physical transmitting of stem cells through the placenta migrating in both directions, i.e., from child to mother, as well as from mother to child. The child carries part of the mother; the mother carries part of the child for decades, if not for some, a lifetime. As one researcher put it: "You live in them, and they live in you."

Consequently, there's a maternal urgency to love one's offspring, to care for patiently, to guard and protect fiercely, and to forgive generously. Scripture echoes, "Can a woman forget her suckling child, that she should have no compassion on the son/daughter of her womb? Even these may forget, yet I will not forget you" (Is 49:15). The teaching here is that the *amma* qualities of urgent love, patient care, fierce protection, and compassion are inborn qualities of biblical mercy, and hence, God's intended meaning. *Divine Mercy* aptly enhances these feminine tones of mercy:

> Souls who spread the honor of My mercy
> I shield through their entire lives as a ten-

OPERATIVE MERCY

der mother her infant, and at the hour of death, I will not be a Judge for them, but a Merciful Savior. (*Diary*, n. 1075)

Write this for the benefit of distressed souls; when a soul sees and realizes the gravity of its sins, when the whole abyss of the misery into which it is immersed itself is displayed before its eyes, let it not despair, but with trust let it throw itself into the arms of My mercy, as a child into the arms of its beloved mother. (*Diary*, n. 1541)

Using *Divine Mercy's* own descriptive words, i.e., "as a tender mother shields her infant" as a starting point, dare we infer that "at the hour of death" rather than meeting a severe "judge," those "who spread the honor" of his divine mercy will discover a welcoming "mothering savior?"

Finally, intricate to this mercy-mix is *hanan*, "a steady predisposition to be good and humane toward others." There is as well *hamal*, highlighting a person's empathetic readiness to spare and remit others of their deserved punishment. Talk about disarming the heart! Although admittedly from another scriptural context, the complaint: "This is intolerable language. How could anyone accept it?" (Jn 6:60), surely seems more than applicable in this context. In other words, when we realize what the Bible is actually teaching us about forgiving mercy, we'd rather turn the page to find something easier to do.

CELEBRATING COMPASSION

These alleviating qualities of *hesed, rahamin, hanan,* and *hamal* each and all help to define what forgiving mercy truly is from a perspective of divine revelation. They must be taken together for forgiving mercy's full identity to be grasped. Another way of stating the same thing is, each and all are required for mercy's integrity. None are incidental. Taking them together makes it evident that forgiving mercy is not a single timely action (e.g., "letting people off the hook") rather forgiving mercy, by its full nature, demands follow-through. This indicates quite well that forgiving mercy is always a sustained process.

For a sense of context here, let's look at the parable of the *Good Samaritan* (Lk 10:29–27). To demonstrate the full measure of mercy, Jesus depicts this Samaritan, not just in his noticing the beaten man in the ditch, not only merely making the decision to put aside his own plans and journey, not only assisting the wounded man with oils/helping up—but mounts the man on his (Samaritan's) own mule and takes the beaten victim to shelter and recuperative care. So this "first responder" is genuinely a concerned "proactive deliverer" away from ditch and dying to cover and care. The Gentile Samaritan even spends the first night attending his patient. But that's still not the end of the Samaritan's compassion. His intention is to accompany the hurting man beyond his immediate medical needs. It's going to require follow-through, without which, the full measure of the Samaritan's mercy will not occur. So he promises to return, to check up on the healing progress of the patient, and to pay whatever his care will entail.

This extended interest and caring points out the readiness/lavishness of God's mercy toward us—that by nature,

OPERATIVE MERCY

it includes full recuperation. It's exactly what Jesus did with Peter after Peter's fearful denial. Just like Jesus with Peter, the Good Samaritan instilled hope; he was not only a rehabilitating but a restorative influence. Therefore—and again, more than just "letting people off the hook"—God's mercy, and the ultimate template of our own mercy toward others, is about dissolving the hook entirely. "Follow-through"— the goal being ongoing, full rehabilitation—cannot occur unless that hook is first dissolved. Otherwise, the hook maintains an entrapping hold on hope.

So the full panoramic expose of biblical mercy is most challenging. Because we are considering the scriptural significance of forgiving mercy, there's much more than a momentary pity suggested here. These qualities of forgiving mercy push us to consider life beyond any personal offense. They "cajole" us to redress hurt with love not injury, i.e., "where there is hatred, let me show love, where there is injury, pardon" (Francis of Assisi). In a spirit of focused empathy, the truly compassionate person strategizes as how to be a creative deliverer. Full-fledged mercy schemes to be an instrument of restoring the offender to honest peace and dignity. We'll come back to this several times.

Our Holy Father Francis is a veritable beacon of hope in this mercy arena. It cannot be by accident but by inspiration of the Holy Spirit that he was chosen at this age and time of the Church and society. The day after his election, among his first words were: "Let's learn to be merciful with everybody. Let's invoke the intercession of the virgin who had in her arms the mercy of God made man" (Angelus, March 14, 2013). He'd been preaching mercy for years.

CELEBRATING COMPASSION

This is the Lord's most powerful message: mercy… Only someone who has encountered mercy, who has been caressed by the tenderness of mercy, is happy and comfortable with the Lord… I dare to say that the privileged locus of the encounter with the Lord is the caress of the mercy of Jesus Christ on my sin…of one who knows me, knows my betrayals and loves me just the same, appreciates me, embraces me, calls me again, hopes in me, and expects from me. (Francis, Buenos Aires, 1999)

Three days later, on March 17, at St. Peter's Square, he spoke on Jesus' "Forgiveness of the Adulterous Woman" (Jn 8:1–13). Listen for the *abba-amma* shades of compassion.

Jesus' attitude is striking; we do not hear words of scorn, we do not hear words of condemnation, but only words of love, of mercy, that invite us to conversion… he forgets. He has a very special capacity for forgetting. He forgets, he kisses you, he embraces you, and he simply says, "Neither do I condemn you, go and sin no more!" The Lord never tires of forgiving us, never! Well, brothers and sisters, the face of God is that merciful father, who always has patience. Let us remember the prophet Isaiah, who says that even if our sins are bright red, God's mercy can make them white as snow. Mercy is beautiful!

Mercy's Amnesty

If Pope Francis says, "Mercy is about forgetting, God forgets," John Cardinal Onaiyekan, archbishop of Abuja, put it this way:

> Pardon, forgiveness, and amnesty belong to the divine. Of course, God is just but he is also merciful. It is precisely through the omnipotence of God that he can reconcile his justice with his mercy. The Old Testament says clearly that God shows his almighty power above all his mercy, offering a forgiveness that wipes out our offenses as if they never took place. (2013 Easter Message, *God's Mercy and Human Pardon*)

Satanic Tabulator

The only one who does not forget is Satan. He meticulously tabulates and keeps scrupulous tract in his book of death of every single weakness and sin ever committed by any individual—and he'll use it when and as it fits his demonic dreams. A family, a spouse, a town, a society, a church community, which cannot let go of other's past mistakes/sinfulness—especially of decades ago—honestly hasn't even minimally forgiven or been about God's

CELEBRATING COMPASSION

mercy, no matter the rhetoric. This is especially so when the offender has unmistakably repented, completed penance and reparation, and presently lives truly in the graces of God. More accurately, therefore, genuine mercy sends and accompanies the forgiven person back into the challenge of life. The repentant person being wiser, more experienced, converted, there is every indication and trust that s/he will lead a changed life consistently. Holistic mercy insists on just such an opportunity, otherwise the forgiven is sent back to life in a depressive, if not despairing shroud of blameful history.

Once offended, it's relatively easy to choke off any thoughts of forgiving the offender and to simply harbor resentment, hate, bitterness, and revenge. Such emotions are very easy not only to sustain but to embellish. The temptation is to label and define others by their offenses and mistakes. Then if we're not careful, the challenge is to defend our labels and definitions of others for the rest of their lives—and ours!

On the contrary, honest maturing mercy requires intentionally tempered courage. The path to being merciful is not for vacillators. Efficacious mercy requires consciously determined fortitude. Persevering mercy requires serious depths of resolute inner strength. Committed mercy takes resolved decision. Mercy doesn't mean you don't address the problem, but mercy projects a hope, an alleviation within life beyond the confrontation. The person finding difficulty in being a forgiver needs to imagine and project what life could be once forgiveness has taken place. This is especially so when a person has difficulty forgiving one's self!

The person who has the possibility to be merciful is, by that fact, a decidedly privileged individual. To be authentic, mercy has to be offered freely, not out of any exterior pressure or decree (e.g., "you two shake hands and make up!"), rather it emerges from a big heartedness, not burden. It reveals an all-encompassing benevolence, a joyful and ready willingness to do genuine good to another, to alleviate rather than to harm. It's precisely that magnanimity and altruism of heart from which clemency and compassion naturally arise. Goodness of heart flows from sincere love simply because honest love is by nature effusive. In other words, it has an inborn urgency to share, to give of oneself in favor of another, even to the point of sacrifice rather than to take from another. It has an inborn earnestness to be compassionate. Because *hesed, rahamin, hanan,* and *hamal* all have adamant, enduring qualities about them, they do not describe a momentary half-hearted, retractable, or just for-the-occasion sentiment. For this reason, they are particularly identified with and applicable to God.

Mercy's Essential Conditions

So what qualities are essential conditions of true mercy—anyone's mercy? What's the motive behind all motives, especially God's mercy? Unequivocally, the response is proactive love—a proactive, divine love at that. God's fidelity to the divine essence of love impels God's mercy. "But God, who is rich in mercy, out of great love with which he loved us, even when we were dead through our trespasses, made us alive in Christ" (Eph 2:4). "God is love" (1 Jn 4:16), and mercy is "as it were love's second name" (John Paul II, *Dives in Misericordia*, n. 7).

No matter the provocation, true love strenuously ostracizes any possibility of unmitigated hate, revengeful retaliation, or "getting even"—which is often some people's definition of "justice." "The only people with whom you should try to get even are those who have helped you" (John E. Southard). Genuine love rightfully purges the very impetuous thought of revenge or unwillingness to forgive.

A second motive underpinning all mercy is the awareness that compassion toward others is an absolute condition of one's own interior healing and peace. Even God chooses to assuage divine woundedness and rejection by a letting go—a forgetting. Again the first one to heal, the first one to be set free of any burden due to personal hurt, is the forgiver.

Divine Amnesia

A third concomitant quality of that love just has to be a divine humility, evidenced in a willingness to put up with the likes of us, caressing us, and washing us clean. God's mercy is—as John Cardinal Onaiyekan preached—about a "divine amnesty." We could even say it's a divine amnesia which includes not only willful forgetfulness of our offending action but of the personal rejection experienced.

> But if the wicked turn away from all
> their sins that they have committed and
> keep all my statutes and do what is law-
> ful and right, they shall surely live, they

shall not die. None of the transgressions that they have committed shall be remembered against them; for the righteousness that they have done they shall live. (Ezek. 18:21–22)

At times, unwillingness to forgive is not only undergirded by an agitated ego but even more indicatively by a feebleness of soul. The inability or reluctance to forgive seeps into one's entire spirituality. Unless addressed, there it will fester. Depending upon its adamancy, non-forgiveness is a proportionate barrier to deeper relationship with God. In other words, it's a hindrance because it is not of the mind, heart, and example of Jesus. Forgiving has less to do with what's reasonable than it does with reclaiming and redirecting a wounded heart. Forgiving has to do with the caliber, i.e., with the vulnerability of one's relationship with God, as well as with who one chooses to be and become as celebration of that relationship. Forgiving has to do with responding to God's invitation to become Christlike.

A fourth consideration to nourish ongoing mercy is—as Pope Francis indicates—patience. The key here is found in the passage: "But God proves his love for us that while we still were sinners Christ died for us" (Rom 5:8). In other words, even while we are sinners, a waiting, hopeful God still loves us and, consequently, is prepared to wait for our conversion. Scripture echoes: "Love is patient… It does not rejoice in wrongdoing but rejoices in the truth. It bears all things…hopes all things, endures all things" (1 Cor 13:4–7).

CELEBRATING COMPASSION

These four essential qualities of mercy (i.e., proactive love, seeking one's own peace, humility, and patience) are critical assets and conditions of anyone's mercy. Taken together, they contribute to, if not determine, the potential for any forgiving mercy toward others in our own lives. Mercy isn't about what's politically correct or the "safe thing" to do. It's about what is the loving, peace-gaining, freeing, patient, and humble thing to do.

Mercy and Memory

What does mercy require in the one being forgiven? Basically there are two essential qualities of soul needed: sorrow for the offense and resolve not to repeat the wrong. "Neither do I condemn you. Go your way, and from now on do not sin again!" (Jn 8:11). Pope Francis says, "Mercy is about forgetting, God forgets." However, while God forgets, the forgiven offender can never afford to forget. Memory is part and parcel of sorrow, of purpose of amendment, and of ongoing, sustained conversion. It's at the very heart of a determination never to return and repeat the sin—hence, remembering where not to go, what not to do again.

Conscience and Guilt

There is surely a time and a place for appropriate guilt. In the reality of personal sin, pertinent guilt is a first sign that a healthy conscience is working. But rather than the penitent's memory being forever burdened by sustained shame or self-reproach, it's a memory bathed in divine,

28

consoling love and alleviation. Such contrition and conversion, i.e., reassessing one's own attitudes and actions, assures that the person's conscience is rehabilitated due to a change of heart. This calls for a willingness to be remolded, which, in turn, realigns one's vision. The result is an adamant determination to act differently.

God's Defining Feature

God's most defining characteristic is not divine justice but God's bountiful mercy and pardon evidenced primarily in sending an only "beloved son" in the first place. God unmistakably reiterates this through St. Maria Faustina Kowalska (1905–1938) and Divine Mercy: "Proclaim that mercy is the greatest attribute of God. All the works of My hands are crowned with mercy" (*Diary*, n. 301). Benedict XVI wrote: "God's passionate love for his people—for humanity—is at the same time a forgiving love. It is so great that it turns God against himself, his love against his justice" (Benedict XVI, *Deus Caritas Est.*, n. 10).

Redemption's ultimate goal is to usher the wayfaring, at times, sinful pilgrim back to the pristine virtue of paradise. Redemption means being reborn, refinanced in the economy of salvation through the redemptive passion, death, and resurrection of a compassionate messiah. The incarnation and redemption not only deal with the absolute dissolving of sin but necessarily and consequently with recreating the sinner back to innocence. "'Come now, let us argue it out,' says the Lord, 'though your sins are like scarlet, I will make them as white as snow, though they are red like crimson, they shall become like wool'" (Is 1:18).

CELEBRATING COMPASSION

That's the heart of mercy, namely pardon, rehabilitation, and a divine letting go. *No one* is beyond the reach of Divine Mercy in its fullness! That's gospel! It's also St. John Paul II: "No human sin can erase the mercy of God or prevent him from unleashing all his triumphant power, if we only call upon him" (*Veritas Splendor*, n. 118). It's evident that God is *always* ready to holistically forgive. "God is the first to stoop to the sinner" (*Diary*, n. 598).

2

Christic Compassion

Without God's forgiving mercy made alive in Jesus, sin and Satan win.

God's lavish purpose of creating in the first place was to generously share divine benevolence. There's a universal principle: "goodness is effusive," meaning it has an innate urgency to give of itself. Such is God's essence. Despite the momentous failure of our first parents, God sends unmistakable evidence of endless, divine love and hope of living in eternal union with us. God missions a "beloved son" to make evident reparation and to reclaim us. How each of us responds to this "Savior" will be the determining cause of whether or not we share in eternal life. So one of the more important questions a Christian will ever have to answer is the same one Jesus asked Peter: "Who do you say that I am?" An equally important question is: "And how much influence are you going to allow me in your life?"

All four gospel accounts reveal the scuttlebutt going around about Jesus once he began his public ministry.

CELEBRATING COMPASSION

Certain scribes and Pharisees formed their opinions of Jesus. Suspecting and judging him to be a threat to their own brand of Judaism, just another of the false prophets, they felt a need in their hearts to condemn him.

Jesus' "Set Up" Question

But there were also followers of John the Baptist who were part of the so-called "remnant of Israel," who had robust hope that this Jesus of Nazareth was, in fact, their long-awaited Messiah. Among that "remnant" were not only Jesus' mother and her husband, Joseph, but her own parents, and the Baptist's parents as well. There were also the handpicked apostles. Of "the twelve," as they began to be called, Jesus asks one of his setup questions. In other words, Jesus already knows the answer. He wants to raise awareness among those he queries. The question: "What are people saying about me? What's the scuttlebutt? Who do people say I am?"

Jesus wasn't ignorant. He knew quite well what people were saying about him. It was a very mixed bag. For instance, some thought he was the Baptist come back to life or perhaps one of the prophets like Elijah. At the annunciation to Joseph, the angel declares just who this child will be: "You are to name him Jesus because he will save his people from their sins" (Mt 1:21). On numerous occasions, he was addressed as "Master" (Mk 10:51; Lk 5:5, 8:24, 9:33), as "the Holy One of God" (Lk 4:34) by of all creatures, an unclean spirit! But Gabriel had already predicted that title (Lk 1:32). The angel broadcasting Jesus' birth to the astounded shepherds called Jesus "Christ the Lord" (Lk

32

2:11). His neighbors recognized him as a "carpenter" like his dad and as "the son of Mary." Some considered him "Son of God" (Lk 1:23), which title is confirmed when his very own Heavenly Father claims him as "my beloved son" (Mk 1:11, 9:8). Within two sentences, Jesus is called both "the prophet" and "the Messiah" (Jn 7:40–41). Informed and bolstered by grace, Peter weaves together "you are the Christ, the Son of the living God" (Mt 16:16). Later, Jesus would be called "Rabboni" (Jn 20:17), and "my Lord and my God" (Jn 20:28). So far so good. But he would also be negatively branded as "a man who eats with sinners" (Mk 2:15), and more than once, a "blasphemer" (Mt 9:3, 26:65; Mk 2:7, 14:64; Jn 10:36), and hence, a sinner.

Jesus' Self-definition

Interesting enough, amidst that developing gossip and confusion, Jesus had already begun to explain and define himself. Let's just take John's gospel: "I am the Bread of Life" (6:3.5). "I am Light of the World" (8:12, 9:5). "I am the Sheepgate" (10:7). "I am the Good Shepherd" (10:11). "I am the Resurrection and Life" (11:25). "I am the Way, Truth, and Life" (14:6). "I am the Vine" (15:1). "I am the Compassion of God." "Wait a minute," you may immediately respond, "I've never seen that self-definition in scripture. Where exactly does it say that?" The answer, of course, is between every line of the gospel. One of the most recorded, most attractive and predominant images of Jesus throughout the gospel is precisely that of being a most compassionate healer and forgiver.

Jesus: Healer and Forgiver

The title of the optional *Eucharistic Prayer IV for Various Needs* used to be *Jesus the Compassion of God.* Unfortunately, it's been homogenized down to *Jesus, Who Went Around Doing Good.* Quite simply, Jesus is the most evident, in-your-face sign that God empathizes with all types and modes of suffering, physical and mental, emotional and spiritual. Further, he not only agonizes with us, he enters into our experience and is a persevering companion. Being that divine presence personified, Jesus is *the* sacrament of God's limitless love, immeasurable mercy, and compassion. He's both the incomparable act and enactor of divine compassion. Pope Francis, speaking of Jesus, writes:

> From the beginning of his ministry in Galilee, he approached lepers, demoniacs, all the sick and marginalized. Such behavior was in no way usual. So true is this that Jesus' liking for the excluded, the "untouchables," was one of the things that most disconcerted his contemporaries. Wherever there was a person suffering, Jesus took charge of him, and that suffering became his own. Jesus did not preach that the condition of pain should be endured with heroism, in the manner of the stoic philosophers. Jesus shared human pain, and when he came across it, there burst in his innermost being that attitude that characterizes Christianity—mercy.

CHRISTIC COMPASSION

In face of human pain, Jesus feels mercy; Jesus' heart is merciful. Jesus feels compassion, literally he feels his innermost being quiver. How many times in the gospels we encounter reactions of this sort. The heart of Christ incarnates and reveals the heart of God that wherever there is a man or woman suffering, he wills their cure, their liberation, their full life. (Audience *On Divine Mercy, Forgiveness*, August 9, 2017, Zenith)

Why did the thousands gather to listen and to be close to Jesus? What did they discover within his presence, personality, and actions that attracted them? Well, there's a universal principle: "goodness attracts." Jesus not only consistently tells the unacceptable of his day and time, "both my Father and I love you" (Jn 15:9), but proves it beyond any shadow of a doubt through his behavior. When a person hears s/he is loved, s/he immediately also hears s/he is valued. Let's look at the gospel of Luke, which, with reason, is referred to as "the gospel of mercy" (*Dives in Misericordia*, n. 3).

Just as the other three evangelists, Luke records only some of what must have been Jesus' countless physical healings. Surely they must have had resounding resonance not only in the very souls of the cured but equally in those of eyewitnesses. For instance, there is the healing of a single leper (5:12f) and later of ten lepers (17:11f), of paralyzed people (5:17f), the cure of Peter's mother-in-law (4:38f), an unexpressed number of other cures at sunset (4:40f), the

CELEBRATING COMPASSION

deliverance of more than a single demoniac (4:31f, 8:26f, 9:37f, 11:14f), of a man with a withered hand (6:6f), of a Roman official's servant (7:1f), of the hemorrhaging woman who touched his cloak (8:40f), of the man at the pool near the sheepgate, the raising of the dead—e.g., the only son of a widowed mother (7:11f), of Lazarus (Jn 11:1f), of the daughter of Jairus (8:40–42, 49–56). Additionally, there was curing of a crippled woman (13:10f) and of a feeble, dropsical man (14:1f), both on a Sabbath; and of the blind man from Jericho (18:35f).

Compassion's Fuller Picture

Jesus tirelessly exemplified what he himself preached: "Be compassionate as your heavenly father is compassionate" (Lk 6:36). There was his insistence and witness regarding brotherly or sisterly correction: "If your brother or sister does something wrong, reprove him/her, and if s/he is sorry, forgive him/her. And if s/he wrongs you seven times a day and seven times comes back to you and says, 'I am sorry,' you must forgive him/her" (Lk 17:4f).

Secondly, more about soul healing than bodily cures, Jesus' teaching parables arose directly from his compassionate heart, e.g., his three explicit mercy parables that of the lost sheep, the lost coin, and the lost prodigal son (Lk 15f). Not to be left out, there was the generous, if not unguarded mercy of a lavishly doling out landowner toward the shift workers in his vineyard (Mt 20:1f), as well as the demonstrative love and selfless compassion of a good Samaritan (Lk 10.29f).

CHRISTIC COMPASSION

Thirdly, there is Jesus' professed, sympathetic openness to even the unfriendly, in other words, those we find difficult to love: "But I say this to you, love your enemies, do good to those who hate you, bless those who curse you, pray for those who treat you badly" (Lk 6:27f).

Then, of course, his seminal sermon on the mount (Mt 5:1f), the *Magna Carta* of serious discipleship is in every respect couched in lively compassion. In the Last Judgment event (Mt 25:31f) what Jesus predicts is totally, unashamedly about those who have shown proactive compassion—and those who have not—because they could or could not recognize the face, and consequently, honor the person of Jesus in the hungry, the shunned person or family, the ill-clothed wo/man or child, or the confined, shamed prisoner.

Compassion parables are a theme and refrain occasioned by the Pharisees rashly judging Jesus to be a reprobate himself. Why? Because he was seen hanging around with "sinners," even going so far as frequently going to their homes and eating with them (Lk 15:1–3). "Show me your friends, and I'll tell you who you really are!" Jesus left little doubt. He knew exactly how to make press. He realized how to get a headline! Proof of that is when he summons the man with a withered hand to "come out into the middle," i.e., right into the faces of the very scribes and Pharisees who "were watching him to see if he would cure on the Sabbath" (Lk 6:6f).

No shy Savior, this Jesus. He openly and unabashedly, clearly and prophetically took time to reach out to and to be friendly with the seemingly "lost"—the "untouchables," the "shamed" of his day—toward those in serious

CELEBRATING COMPASSION

need of his presence, love, and mercy. No apologies to anyone. Without doubt, he fully intended to display an actual, divine favoritism for them despite their alleged waywardness. After all, he was trying to attract, to heal, and to convert them. That focused compassionate presence, love, and mercy would be the "come on" for the conversion of other sinners, the long-awaited solace of soul for the worldly downtrodden and poor. Compassion and welcome on the part of Jesus are at the heart of his focused ministry. "Come to me all you who labor and are overburdened, and I will give you rest" (Mt 1:28). Jesus knew and lived the psalms. "If you never overlooked our sins, O Lord, could anyone survive?" (Ps 130:3).

> Merciful and gracious is the Lord, slow to anger, abounding in mercy. He will not always accuse, and nurses no lasting anger; He has not dealt with us as our sins merit, nor requited us as our wrongs deserve. For as the heavens tower over the earth, so his mercy towers over those who fear him. As far as the east is from the west, so far has he removed our sins from us. As a father/mother has compassion on his/her children, so the Lord has compassion on those who fear him. For he knows how we are formed, remembers that we are dust. (Ps 103:8–14)

Luke's entire fifteenth chapter of the lost sheep, the lost coin, and the lost son carries the sober theme and refrain of not just being missing but eagerly and happily being sought out until found. These three parables concerning God's mercy dispute any human estimation of how God should—or shouldn't act. The teaching of all three stories is that the so-called "lost"/wayward/self-shackled, the captivated/addicted-to-sin are still operatively and actively pursued—no matter what seems politically incorrect. But to get the full measure of Jesus' teaching, a most important and critical question needs to be asked: "Why? Who really cares when there are—just like the ninety-nine sheep or the nine coins still in hand—so many others who are already saved?" That's pointedly the startling revelation in these parables. It is the salient point of this Christic revelation: God cares! Referring, of course, to that solicitous God, the *Eucharistic Prayer for Masses of Reconciliation I* used to say: "When we were lost and could not find the way to you, you loved us more than ever."

Jesus' Penchant for Sinners

In case anyone missed Jesus' unmistakable penchant for "the sinner" and "the lost," Jesus not only explicitly preached but repeatedly and personally exercised forgiveness. On the occasion of absolving the sins of a remorseful lady washing his feet with her tears, able to read into the more expansive depths of her heart, a compassionate Jesus chose to consider her whole person. Then he gave the reason for extending his mercy: "Her sins, many as they are, shall be forgiven her." Why? "Because she has loved much" (Lk 7:47–50). Jesus grasped the full aura of her humanity, which, in turn, became the very basis of the trust he

CELEBRATING COMPASSION

invested in a conversional, hope-filled second chance for her.

A second chance explicitly implied a returning to life as it was with all its parameters, demands, and possibilities. However, now it would be a life not only purified by the humility of failure but by the still loving, still trusting acceptance and encouragement of Jesus. Seeing beyond her previous sinful choices, Jesus was more impressed with her deeper, still active, enduring love. So rather than terminally prosecuting her offense, he compassionately enveloped the repentant woman within his mercy. Otherwise, her sin would have become the ultimate winner. Mercy tells sin that it (sin) doesn't have the last word!

Jesus chose Peter despite Peter's mistakes. Jesus did not demand an already-confirmed sanctity and perfection. Even more important and beyond Peter's fearful failures of denial, Jesus saw something decent, better, and wiser in Peter. Jesus chose to concentrate on Peter's tested and redeemed love, his tearful humility, his innate dignity and enduring hunger for meaning and holiness of life beyond his failures. He saw the same in Thomas, beyond Thomas's dismay and reservations; in Mary Magdalene, beyond her previous, enmeshed life style; in the woman at the water well, beyond her entangled marital life; in the good thief, beyond his dishonest life choices. Giving us the example of when he says, "Be merciful, just as your Father is merciful" (Lk 23:36), Jesus even forgives his very executioners in the actual act! At the very heartbeat of the Good News is the unswerving message that Jesus chooses to look beyond ours and other's personal, sinful failures, to look beyond to what forgiveness inspires and makes possible—namely renewed,

CHRISTIC COMPASSION

wiser fidelity to his own living embodiment of operative compassion. As he did for the others, Jesus chooses to take into account the totality of our efforts to live, to learn to love despite our passing failures.

By and large, there are great signs of empathetic compassion in today's world, e.g., times of hurricanes, earthquakes, and family death. But if we're both observant and honest, there is also a serious dearth of holistic, forgiving compassion. It's not only in the secular world today but likewise within Christianity itself.

So many of us are still ideologically living in Old Testament times: "an eye for an eye, a tooth for a tooth" (Lev. 24:20), where pure vengeance was/is clothed in a disarming disguise of justice. There seemingly abounds a psychological, spiritual aversion to even think of forgiving another or to ever trust a wrongdoer once a perceived offense has occurred. From where/whom the ironclad claw?

At times, we can be just like the prophet Jonah, a reasonably good man. He was actually a chosen prophet, who, nevertheless, did not want God to forgive the Ninevites, even to the point that he'd rather die before agreeing to God's mercy for them (Jon 4). Were his intentions all purely religious, or were there other factors, e.g., of animosity, prejudice, jealousy, or a hint of self-righteousness going on even within his attained measure of goodness? Evidently, although good and chosen, he was not perfect. He didn't want the Ninevites to change precisely so they could be punished. Either way, he had some obvious emotional baggage manipulating his value system. Just like the older brother of the prodigal son, Jonah needed God's healing to deal with these intransigent obstacles before he him-

CELEBRATING COMPASSION

self could be honestly free and genuinely obedient to the entire divine plan of compassion.

Whether between countries or political ideologies, religion or races, offenders within family or Church, mercy and people's compassion have very often succumbed to righteousness—very often, possibly an unconscious self-righteousness but possibly more often an unwilling-to-admit self-righteousness. Evidently based on personal experience, Faustina prayed this quite insightful prayer to our Blessed Mother: "O Mary, my mother and my lady…defend me with your power against all enemies, and especially against those who hide their malice behind the mask of virtue" (*Diary*, n. 79).

A paramount question: Who or what is an unmerciful, non-compassionate person, society, family, or religion becoming? In other words, what does lack of a compassionate heart do to its "proprietor?" As we've seen in chapter 1, the ultimate aim of justice ought not merely to be measured reparation to and satisfaction for the offended—as integral as these may be—but decisive conversion, a new life, a new heart, and peaceful rehabilitation for all. "Righteousness and peace shall kiss each other" (Ps 85:11). The clear implication is that righteousness and peace have found viable, mutual friendship and love.

When we experience difficulty in summoning a self-liberating forgiveness of others into our own hearts—as many of us may—we need to plead for inner freedom and conversion from the one who verified by life and action: "I am the Compassion of God." That's at least a start. He won't hold back. He knows exactly what to do. He's the fount

CHRISTIC COMPASSION

and fullness of limitless divine mercy. His compassion was energized by that limitless, outgoing love.

Divine Mercy may well begin as an appealing devotion or be referred to as "a movement." But once vulnerably embraced, what seemed like a mere pietistic devotion or even a compelling movement becomes an urgent way of life, Jesus being its protagonist push and pulse.

Who do you say I am? This question is not actually nor ultimately answered by quoting the explanations of Jesus by others or even by his own self-definitions. The only honest response is given by the way we actually live our lives.

3

Abba Mercy

Check out the daily news. The world is inundated with hurt, obsession for power, and "getting even" with others. A major part of the world seems immersed in uncontrolled confrontation in Old Testament retaliatory times of "an eye for an eye" (Lev. 24:20). There is so much hate and violence in responding to injury. Clearly, there's a frightening famine of genuine true love in today's world, consequently no viable place or possibility allowed for forgiving love and mercy.

Mercy's Caressing

Rabbi Jesus not only taught but gave personal and explicit witness to some shocking truths about compassion and forgiveness: "Turn the other cheek" (Lk 6:29). "Seventy times seven" (Mt 18:21). "If you do not forgive others, neither will your Heavenly Father forgive your trespasses" (Mt 6:15). "If s/he says, 'I repent,' you must forgive" (Lk 16:4). So Jesus raised a lot of irate eyebrows! He turned many

44

people off! They covered their ears. They tore their garments in staunch, showy disagreement. So when—in the spirit of Jesus—Pope Francis describes forgiving mercy in terms of "a caressing, a kissing, a forgetting," in somewhat the same mood as scribes and Pharisees, everything in the gut of those who hurt vehemently revolts. Their wounds rise up in defense and rebellion. The very notion of compassion is not only unspeakable but unthinkable. So from where does Pope Francis get his depicting of mercy?

When reflecting upon the theme of forgiving mercy, Jesus' account of the prodigal son (Lk 15:11–32) is without equal. The disarming reactions of a wounded, grieving father strike at the very sinews of our hearts, unless, of course, our hearts have already turned to stone. With deliberate detail, Jesus is actually describing the inner workings of divine mercy toward a sinner. Understandably, the humble, unreserved clemency on the part of the father is what is more often preached and written about. But there's an important subplot which runs throughout. It's about a hyped, self-righteous jealousy—actually, a fraternal contempt on the part of an older son. In his opinion, his father's preposterous willingness to forgive the reckless younger brother is undeniably ill-advised. The intended Christic teaching here is that it's precisely the contempt and self-righteousness of the older son which makes mercy so unthinkable for him.

Mercy's verses Self-righteousness

Jesus portrays a very faithful, hardworking, older son emerging from the field worn out when he notices some

CELEBRATING COMPASSION

unexpected activity going on. He hears music. There's dancing. There's a barbecue being prepared. When he asks what's going on, he gets aggravating news: "Your brother has returned!" If we pick up the full tone of the parable, the big brother's reaction is not just "oh my gosh! What's he doing back?" But more like "what in the hell is he doing here!" So aware of what's going on, he's furious. After all, he's been the upright, faithful, and dependable son. But here's the problem: In this instance, it's his personal brand of self-righteousness that inoculates his heart against the slightest fraternal compassion. Attitudinally, he's exiled his brother beyond any possibility of family exoneration. Letting his emotions get the better of him, he attempts to dictate what his evidently misguided, naive father shouldn't/can't do! Totally self-centered in this instance, he transposes mercy ministered to his brother into a personal affront to himself.

But notice well, there's another intended, unavoidable teaching of Jesus. Even under severe in-house pressure, the *abba* doesn't for an instant change his mind or back off one iota. He neither apologizes nor waters down his unreserved compassion and absolution. His *abba* love is stable and unbending. Not for one moment does he sheepishly succumb to the vociferous clamor of his first born. Knowing and owning who he himself is, the daddy staunchly and prophetically stands his chosen and determined ground. The teaching: that extending mercy to another, will, at times, call for adamant, if not prophetic courage. Even in the face of staunch, filial rebuttal, the father remains most patient, meek, and merciful with his older complaining son. He pleads with him in equally loving and compassion-

46

ate terms, "My son, you are here always." Then the *abba* gives the motive behind his own joyous decision, "But your brother was dead and has come to life again. He was lost and has been found." Now it's up to the older son to accept or to continue rejecting, but it won't change the father.

Now let's not miss this important point. Just like his younger brother, against whom he seems to have so much animosity for lustful and greedy failures, the older son—as good as he is—has his own lingering failures. He's jealous. Consequently, he, too, desperately needs a healing conversion to be brought to a fuller life of virtue, personal peace, and freedom.

Interface this parable of *abba* mercy with that of the shift workers in the vineyard and the owner's more than just remuneration (Mt 20:1–6). Like with the older son, contention enters the picture when those who have worked longer judge that the manager acts in defiance of their own sweated out, merited wage. They, too, get vociferously angry at his generous payment. But just like the *abba*, the boss doesn't back down, apologize, nor try to appease either. Hearing the laborers envious complaints, the owner candidly asks of just what they are accusing him, "What injustice have I done? Have I no right to do what I like with my own money? Why be envious because I am generous?" We can immediately paraphrase: "Why be envious because I am merciful?"

Let's go back to consider those captivating actions of an affronted yet still compassionate father. There are some commonalities of attitude and action in both father and delinquent son. For instance, there's been a protracted emptiness, a sorrowful longing going on within the dad.

He genuinely misses his son. Think about it, missing innately carries within it a hope of a returning presence. Otherwise, what's "missing" about? That quality of missing is picked up with the daddy scanning the horizon. Why would he be out there looking? For what? For whom? So longing bespeaks a heartfelt desire for realities to be different—actually spelling out those preferred realities in one's imagination and mind. There's an impatient waiting going on, which hints at a viable openness to a welcoming back, should the occasion arise.

The wasteful son's attitude was equally one of missing but not as a missing of his father. The young man lacks funds, food, and frivolity. These alarming, purely mundane deprivations are what initially seize his attention. They are what slap his conscience into waking up. They cajole him to rethink and to realign his behavior. The moral: God can use anything to move and call us to healing.

Mercy's Symbols: Robe, Ring, and Sandals

Back to the parable, this is the dad's ungrateful, thoughtless, contriving, and using son! Even so, without the slightest hint of lingering retribution or revenge toward his wayward son, the celebrating father excitedly calls out for "the best robe...a ring and sandals." Pointedly, the Lord doesn't include these symbols for nothing.

First of all, a robe—being a full garment—is most significant! It's an outward garment. That's precisely where its symbolism comes from. It covers not only his whole body but what's within. In other words, it's a symbol of what has holistically taken place within the heart and soul of the younger son. It recognizes the core transformation that's occurred inside, i.e., his conversion and repentance, and a thoroughly reconciling grace. It indicates a fundamentally changed, inner life, an authentic recreation for and within the son. Further, it represents the out-and-out disappearance, a letting go of the son's errant behavior in the mind and heart of his father—and it's all the father's idea. "The best robe" is also what others will see—namely not the historical egoism but a purified heart. All true mercy instills and sponsors new life and purpose as we've seen in chapter 1.

The "ring and sandals" each add to the meaning of this mercy ritual. The sandals are to support his son walking a reestablished, wiser journey of life. The ring will be an obvious enduring reminder of his father's stable compassion. So the daddy's evident actions reinstate his son back into full family life and participation. He is not conditionally accepted as one of the hired hands nor sent to the barn in shame. After all, how could any penitent actually witness to a change of life if not fully readmitted, i.e., given a renewed freedom and responsibility. Such witnessing would be impossible if confined to the isolation of a barn. Pope Francis agrees: "The Lord is a master of reintegration. He takes us by the hand and brings us back into the community" (Vatican City, June 21, 2014, Catholic News Agency).

Mercy's Human Dignity

Pope Francis says, "God's mercy gives man life. It brings him back from death." Referring to the privileged time of being merciful, the late Francis Cardinal George,

CELEBRATING COMPASSION

OMI, wrote: "We restore people to their proper dignity and establish our own dignity as well." In other words, genuine mercy conveys to a remorseful heart: "Your failures do not define you, unless you choose them to do so. But despite those failures, you are still lovable. You still have worth and value." Genuine forgiving mercy strengthens a weak wayfarer to move from degrading darkness to promising light. Genuine mercy stretches a healing hand down into the sinkhole of despair in order to assist a penitent in his/her climb out to new life. Genuine mercy affirms a sinner's resurrection from death to life.

Based on Jesus' parable of the prodigal son, which depicts such an empathetic *abba,* there is absolutely no doubt that the merciful Christ stands in staunch, prophetic defense of any truly repentant sinner. With *abba* mercy, there's a readiness, an immediacy in Jesus' mercy—no waiting, no delay. As we've just recalled, there was none whatsoever with the prodigal son, none with the woman taken in adultery, simply "go and sin no more" (Jn 8:1–11). With the "Good Thief," the Lord testifies: "Today" (Lk 23:43), not "after you pay for all your sins in purgatory—maybe!" Neither was there any delay or hesitation with a denying, though repentant, weeping Peter. Jesus simply asks: "Simon, son of John, do you love me?" Peter responding, "Yes, Lord, you know that I love you," Jesus takes Peter at his humbler word. Being reassured, evidently again trusting Peter without hesitation, Jesus fully restores Peter: "Feed my lambs…feed my sheep" (Jn 21:13–17).

Mercy's Risk

No form of mercy is without risks. Not even *abba* mercy has absolute certitude, i.e., that the offender will never repeat the very offense forgiven. Mercy carefully examines that possibility. However, when there are clear signs of there already being "go and sin no more," it opts to mitigate and transform risk into trust. Such is the existential risk involved in extending any mercy—even *abba* mercy. The fecund hope of mercy is that the very act of extending trust and forgiveness becomes, in turn, the precise impetus for open-ended, sustained transformation within the forgiven.

Abba Mercy Resume

So *abba* mercy does not deny the wrong of an offense. Quite the contrary, in fact, mercy has to stare hurt and offense straight in the eye and to put a name on them. But while not at all disregarding the sacredness of directive laws and moral codes, a*bba* mercy consciously pierces through those laws and codes. Forgiving mercy looks to the tested, hopefully wiser humanity of the once offending individual or group in search of fresh and lasting, redeeming qualities. Enlivened with such hope, a*bba* mercy, steeped in every quality of *hesed* mercy (cf. chapter 1), seeks to heal, to rebuild, to strengthen, to reinvigorate, and to realign weak or failed, misguided virtue. *Abba* mercy focuses on transformed life and its possibilities rather than on past weaknesses. It remits deserved punishment (cf. *hamal*, chapter 1). *Abba* mercy innately sponsors holistic resurrection.

CELEBRATING COMPASSION

Abba mercy is what can happen after and because justice has been adequately addressed. St. John Paul II wrote in *Rich in Mercy* (n.7):

> Justice is based on love, flows from it, and tends toward it. Justice is not enough to conquer evil. The answer lies in a justice that is transformed into mercy. True mercy is, so to speak, the most profound source of justice.

While justice has inherent rights founded on legitimate law and obligation, *abba* mercy has its own inborn urgency founded on an eager, acquitting, fecund love.

Abba mercy is a divine elixir for true interior peace not only for the forgiven but equally for the forgiver. It thrives on the scripture: "There will be more rejoicing in heaven over one repentant sinner than over ninety-nine virtuous wo/men who have no need of repentance" (Lk 15:7). The teaching is that the *alleluia* joy of heaven begins at the very summit, i.e., with God.

Finally, though the prodigal son parable sets up an *abba* mercy reflection, it in no way limits its qualities to the male gender. What is said of *abba* mercy is not only compatible with but is one with *amma*, womb mercy, and vice-versa.

4

The Why of Mercy

An elder American Indian brave was trying to teach his young grandson how to deal with the competing tensions between the good and evil we all have to confront in our lives. To impress the boy, he describes two wolves locked in ongoing combat inside each of us. One wolf—very fierce and wicked, even though very cunning—is unable to disguise its anger and desire to get even with others. It can't hide its envy of others. It thrives on self-importance, arrogant conceit, and lavishes unbending control over others. On the contrary, the other engaging wolf is especially good. It doesn't attempt to hide its genuine and happy love for others. It exudes inner strength and peace. It prizes forgiveness of others, even encouraging the fallen with generosity, truth, hope, and fidelity. The mesmerized boy—totally captivated by this very tense scenario—exuberantly asks, "Grandpa, which one wins?" Right to the point, his shrewd teacher replies, "The one you feed!"

Two Vying Spirits

Theology, spirituality, and experience all hold a most important truth: two vying spirits enter all pain and suffering. There is, first of all, the proven compassionate spirit of Jesus. He knew thoroughly the outer limits of pain and betrayal, agony and victimhood. He experienced the bitter gall of rejection beyond our human capacity to fathom. So he knows pain in detail from the inside. This wounded Christ stays present within us for one reason: to accompany, support, and purify us. He stays faithful, carrying us in and through our own suffering to the other side of honest peace and lasting total healing. The sufferer is transformed for the better.

But beware! Concomitantly enters the vindictive, entrapping spirit of Satan—the arrogant wolf—who champions: "Get even, strike back! Never forgive! Never forget! Make them pay! They deserve it! Curse them! Condemn, hate, and publicly malign them if at all possible! Make them say they're sorry first!"

So it's evident, the so-called "prince of darkness" is there also to purposefully accompany us with an intensely focused agenda. That agenda is to instill and to excite confusion into some already distressing issues of heart and soul; to stymie the slightest inclination toward healing, pardon, and operative mercy; to embolden and ratchet up the pained emotions.

Consequently, serious and knowledgeable discernment of spirits, the good from the evil, is paramount. "It is not every spirit, my dear people, that you can trust; test them, to see if they come from God, there are many false proph-

THE WHY OF MERCY

ets now in the world" (1 Jn 4:1). At times, there may be a clear call for substantive penance and sustained prayers for protection against any evil influence for all who are under the pressure of suffering and pain.

For some people, just a thought of forgiving carries heavy emotional baggage. Pardoning another would be an undeniable weakness—humiliating! It smacks of a "giving in to." So what's evidenced to others is a "got-to-save-face bravado" of being undauntedly unforgiving. However, such aversion to exercising mercy fosters illusion. Of what? Of being in charge, of having control over, and of getting even with an offender.

Due to the intense, emotional wounds involved in all hurt, some people find it simply impossible to forgive their offenders. Uncompromisingly, just like the still imperfect Jonah in reference to the Ninevites we read about in chapter 2, they don't want God to forgive their wrongdoers either. Rather and without apology, they'd prefer their offenders to be cast into the deepest fires of hell for all eternity—and in the meantime—no human consolations for them either! In other words, jettisoning their Christian spirituality to the sidelines, they are trying their best to make God into *their own* image and likeness.

But here's something to consider, especially when considerable time, if not years, has passed: it's quite possible that the "perpetrator" has, by now, genuinely repented. God has already forgiven him/her. S/he is already at a redeemed peace. Redemption has already taken place. The person behind the original hurt may be well along a stable path to honest holiness. After all, the journey from sinner to saint is not at all dependent upon nor stymied by others' withheld forgiveness. The personal problem for the one tending to never forgive is that refusal, procrastination, fear to forgive don't allow one's own hurting self to move on. There's an irritating millstone being allowed to hang around one's own heart and person and is being vigilantly fed, guarded, and protected.

Historical Jesus and Mercy

However, it is crystal clear in the scriptures. Jesus stands in devoted protection of any genuinely repentant sinner. After all, he died for them! The unforgiving person, who still hopes to enter heaven, is going to have to reconcile with this truth as an absolute condition for admittance. Based on the incarnate preaching and example of Jesus, there is no sin nor category of sins, which are patently non-forgivable except one—non-forgiveness! Why? Because non-forgiveness inherently negates the very purpose and mission of Jesus, who—as we reflected upon in chapter 2, is "the Compassion of God." For that distinct reason, refusing to be merciful is one of the more serious obstacles to a genuine, maturing relationship with God. "Bear with one another, and if anyone has complaint against another, forgive each other, just as the Lord has forgiven you, so you also must forgive" (Col 3:13).

The why of mercy is found in an unavoidable, intricate weave of spiritual, psychological, and emotional tugs. When we are outraged, looking for "justice," perhaps full of fortified pride and various levels of hopeful retaliation and "payback time," we can conveniently block out what Jesus himself preached, "Be merciful, just as your Father is

THE WHY OF MERCY

merciful. Forgive and you will be forgiven. For the measure with which you measure will in turn be measured out to you" (Lk 6:36–38). "Whoever is angry with his brother/ sister will be liable to judgment" (Mt 5:22). "If you forgive wo/men their transgressions, your heavenly Father will forgive you. But if you do not forgive wo/men, neither will your Father forgive your transgressions" (Mt 6:7–15). "But I say to you, whoever is angry with his brother/sister will be liable to judgment" (Mt 5:22).

Further, when outraged, we can handily dilute the second part of the Our Father's petition: "Forgive us our debts as we also have forgiven our debtors" (Mt 6:12). That small, seemingly unassuming, two-letter word, that simple qualifier "as" is not so innocent. In fact, it's dangerous! It's both the condition, and hence the determinant of just how—or even whether—we are eligible for the divine pardon we ask for ourselves. It's all based, after all, on our own actual forgiving or unforgiving dispositions and witness. It's a mirror word, asking God to reflect back to us the exact image of what we ourselves reveal in our personal behavior.

"Merciless is the judgment on the wo/man who has not shown mercy" (1 Jn 3:15). The Lord cautions us of this very thing in the parable of the fully exonerated but then hard-nosed, intolerant steward who goes out and refuses to be equally compassionate with his fellow servant. Jesus' parable cuts right to the chase: "You wicked servant… I cancelled all that debt of yours when you appealed to me. Were you not bound then to have pity on your fellow servant just as I had pity on you?" (Mt 18:23–35). Somewhere within these teachings, there ought to humbly echo: "Lord, if you count all our [own] iniquities, who could stand?" (Ps

130:3). "Let anyone among you who is without sin be the first to throw a stone" (Jn 8:7). "But God proves his love for us in that [even] while we still were sinners Christ died for us" (Rom 5:8).

As "the Compassion of God," Jesus made divine willingness to forgive a clear and prophetic teaching. Pope Francis teaches: "There is no sin that God cannot forgive! None!" This is an absolute truth! The problem is we human beings and institutions! It's we who can't/won't/don't forgive. The inspirational movie, *I Can Only Imagine*, had a singularly instructive scene and moment of mutual suffering between and within both father and son. It occurs when a genuinely remorseful father is pleading for forgiveness from his son. Why? Because without it, the dad can in no way believe— much less experience—he is forgiven by God. So the dad pleads something along the lines of "why can't God forgive me as he does others? Why can't I have a second chance?" To which the son replies, "God does forgive you. I don't!" Bingo! Evidently, honest words, but no sadder words, no more self-convicting words can ever be spoken by any of us. Who was suffering from what? And why? It was the father's deep pain which became the occasion of his own conversion. The son, who's also in horrific pain, needs more time to learn from his own suffering—his unwillingness to forgive being one major cause. By the grace of God, eventually he learns exactly that and is set free. Until then, like the oldest brother of the prodigal son, who was the bound-up, self-imposed sufferer here? "There's a hard law that when a deep injury is done to us, we never recover until we forgive" (Alan Paton's *Too Late the Phalarope*, 1953).

Pointed questions: how often can I admit to the identical wound of that unforgiving son in my own life? How and why do we who have been offended—okay, maybe seriously—think we need to deny forgiveness to our offenders as an unmistakable sign of our hurt, i.e., as an intentional sign of our eye for an eye? Further maybe embarrassing questions might be: anyone in my own life I need to forgive? Have I ever humbly reached out to him/her? The counter question is: anyone in my own life from whom I need forgiveness? Have I ever asked or conveyed my sorrow to him/her?

Forgiving Mercy and Personal Peace

Why opt to be merciful and forgive offenders? Because not only is forgiveness clearly the Christlike thing to do, it is the womb of personal peace. Christlikeness and personal peace are birthed together. Christlikeness is the effecting cause of our personal peace. Further, being made into the living image of a merciful God, being merciful is more natural to our lives than is rancorous blaming others. Besides that and a true shock for many, forgiving others is actually self-liberating. One's own interior peace is a major reward when exonerating another. Not forgiving is what ensnares us in an unsettled past. Prolonged non-forgiveness is a forbidding symptom of spiritual constipation. In other words, there's a good chance that there are other areas of life underpinning the non-forgiveness which also need attention, e.g., serious lack of self-esteem and personal worth; an unbending need to be in control, a minimal prayer life, i.e., not leaving God in—much less, a compassionate God; a

CELEBRATING COMPASSION

controlled desire to be Christlike; and very possibly unconsciously the seeming choice to love only perfect people.

Non-forgiveness winds up being a self-imposed punishment. Christ-inspired clemency flushes away that enslaving baggage. Returning to the past in order to pardon another is, at the very least, to plant the seed of mercy. The self-inflicted bind of resentment begins to be severed, releasing a life-giving grace for both forgiver and forgiven. But again, the first one set free by extending mercy is the forgiver! Once we extend to others the very merciful benevolence God has extended to us, we are never the same. When finding sustained difficulty in forgiving another, a pertinent question might be: has being unforgiving brought me any lasting genuine tranquility? If not, maybe it's time to try mercy.

Mercy's Demonic Foe

But have no doubt, sacred scripture also warns us about Satan, that second wolf, that "roaring lion" (1 Pet. 5:8). He's further identified as "a liar and the father of lies" (Jn 8:44) who invokes upheaval within our person, our family, our church, and our society. He fosters injustice, hate, confusion, exaggeration, false accusation, division, public, or familial shaming if possible, and very especially a stubborn refusal, a stagnant unwillingness to forgive—all in imitation of himself!

There always seems to be someone who prides self in remembering other peoples' past weaknesses in vivid detail. It's not all that difficult with electronic memory banks. But here's the critical spiritual question: is public revela-

THE WHY OF MERCY

tion of others' misdeeds truly of God's urging? The whole dynamic frenzy of digging up someone else's past—is this even possibly of divine mercy? After all, not all memory is worth remembering. Not all memory is wisdom—but especially so when recall is about tear-down time, when reminiscence is soaked through with vindictiveness. Very interestingly, Faustina's mother general wrote: "Mercy is a beautiful thing, and it must be a great work of the Lord, since Satan opposes it so much and wants to destroy it" (*Diary*, n. 1115). St. Paul writes: "As for my forgiving anything—if there has been anything to be forgiven, I have forgiven it for your sake in the presence of Christ. And so we will not be outwitted by Satan—we know well enough what his intentions are" (2 Cor 2:10–11).

Wounded persons ready to try a fresh road of forgiveness need to be on the alert for groups or individuals who promote and encourage sustained bitterness and revenge, promising some type of satisfying consolation prize and healing peace as a result. An unaddressed anger or festering bitterness remains just that, i.e., unaddressed and festering, and painfully throbbing away, tearfully awaiting a shift of attention for healing. The only delivering salve is forgiveness. Besides that, if we wait until someone else says they're sorry before we choose to forgive them, don't we make ourselves quite dependent upon them? Aren't we allowing them to determine who we choose to be? Who is in control of whom? But that's our choice.

Mercy and Justice

So often hurting people, in lieu of mercy, cry out for justice. That's because justice has a natural ring to it about "an eye for an eye and a tooth for a tooth." That's probably where the phrase "getting even" arises. There are those who believe that by definition and necessity, justice is in an unbending and direct opposition to mercy. Such need not be the case. In a monthly catechesis on divine mercy entitled, *We Have Found Mercy: The Mystery of God's Merciful Love*, Christopher Cardinal Schönborn of Vienna said, "Mercy must be greater than justice. Without mercy, justice itself becomes injustice. It leads to judgment." John Paul II wrote of mercy as not only being "more powerful than justice but more profound." Why? Because "love [the birthing gene of mercy] is greater than justice, i.e., greater in the sense that it is primary and fundamental. Love... conditions justice, and in the final analysis, justice serves love" (*Rich in Mercy*, n. 4). Like fire tempers steel, burning away compromising impurities, mercy tempers justice, and by so doing, strengthens it.

Honest, human love—parental, spousal, and genuine friendship—innately disarms, recalibrates the inner churning demands of justice. That's the "what" and the "how" of love's tempering. True, mature, Christian love opts, and hence, strategizes to hold any retaliatory demons at bay. Justice—if exclusively measured by the fixed, merely human terms and limitations of contracts and statutes, codes, and agreements—can easily slip into the inhumane and hence into the ungodly. This is even more possible, given the pressures of biases, woundedness, and hurt. Non-forgiveness

THE WHY OF MERCY

is not only spiritually but both psychologically and physically unhealthy. The cancer of anger, the poison of hate, the ulcer of revenge, if not treated, inevitably demand their toll from within the total person—soul, body, and mind. Any physician, psychologist, or spiritual director worth his/her salt would readily agree. Mercy is the sole remedy.

"God is love" (1 Jn 4:16) can rightly be translated "God is mercy." Together as one, they epitomize and define God. God's love-mercy is a symbiotic reality belonging to the divine essence and character. Based on this intrinsic union, a human justice—whether of society, Church, or individual, which hasn't taken a sound measure of love-mercy into consideration, by that wanting absence—is a justice which limps. It's an impostor, "a noisy gong or a clanging cymbal" (1 Cor 13:1). How often must Christ still weep because of the lack of mercy and forgiveness in today's world! Mercy and forgiveness are at the Christ-centered heart of the gospel. Consequently, forgiving mercy needs to be at the very heart of anyone who claims to be a Christian.

The biblical revelation, "there is more joy in heaven over the one sinner who repents" (Lk 15:10), ought to be the tip off of the God-intended celebration resulting from our conversion and forgiveness. Heaven holds no grudges! Forgiveness of others is a mature choice. It's actually a noble, indisputable sign of wisdom and freedom.

Forgiving another can be demanding and painful. But forgiving another is to personal peace, what surgery is to removing a cancerous growth. While there is pain involved in the procedure, there's been pain already present for some time. We can choose to continue living with that anguish, or we can choose to confront it and do something about

CELEBRATING COMPASSION

it. Again, our choice! The healing outcome and personal peace are what are chosen. In either scenario, it's a medicinal suffering, i.e., though necessary, it's but temporary and alleviating.

St. Philip Neri spoke wisely when he said, "Who continues in anger, strife, and a bitter spirit has a taste of the air of hell." Hate bitterly connives to ostracize love; Satan furtively conspires to exclude God. No active hater will get to heaven, unless s/he decisively relinquishes his/her animosity to the welcoming, healing heart of divine mercy. "Our hearts can be a sea of mercy and forgiveness to others. This is a very great shortcut to God's heart" (Servant of God, Catherine de Hueck Doherty). "Love everyone out of love for Me, even your greatest enemies so that My mercy may be fully reflected in your heart" (*Diary*, n. 1695).

Mercy for the Love of Christ

Forgiveness is primarily the forgiver's workshop. Being able to pardon others is a clear sign of another enabling presence within, namely Christ's. If you want mercy and peace, contribute to mercy and peace. Don't stand in the way of another's peace because such obstinacy effectively thwarts one's own peace. Forgiveness, if it's not for the love of an individual, how about in discipleship and witness of Christ's love? Once enacted, discipleship and witness can only grow. Christ will enlarge our hearts. Certain people may well claim: "But I've suffered this or that because of another! Why should I forgive?" Jesus assumed unto himself *all* the sins of *all* humanity since the first sin in the Garden of Eden—including mine! Yet he still loved us and

THE WHY OF MERCY

was still willing to forgive us! With such personal benefit as Christians, there ought to be nothing we can't or are unwilling to forgive.

A Time for Building Bridges

There's a time for loving and a time for embracing.
There's a time for throwing all past stones away.
There's a time for healing and a time for forgiving.
There's a time for building bridges, and that time is now.

Chorus:
Oh, take our hearts, Lord, take our minds.
Take our hands, Lord, and make them one.
Take our hearts, Lord, take our minds.
Take our hands, Lord, and make them one.

There's a time for renewing and a time for reconciling.
There's a time for binding up the wounds of the years.
There's a time for planting and a time for sowing.
There's a time for growing the seeds of unity.

(This is a musical meditation on Ecclesiastes 3: 1-8 written by Rev. Carey Landry and published through North American Liturgy Resources, 10802 N. 23rd Ave., Phoenix, Az 85029; copyright 1975. Glory and Praise. pp. 144.)

5

How to Be Merciful?

There is the false slogan: "Time heals all wounds." It's false because by itself it is incomplete and ultimately proffers a baseless hope. Time heals all wounds *if* we operatively desire to be genuinely healed. Time heals all wounds *if* we are willing to personally deal with some things in our lives, in our hearts, and in our minds.

Often, people want personal healing but strictly on their own terms and conditions. They crave interior peace but refuse to let go of the agitated, sometimes hateful, venomous, and revengeful feelings housed and guarded within themselves against spouse, child, parent, judge, or priest. For instance, often enough, people think they will obtain personal healing and peace when their offender is made "to pay up," to suffer publicly if at all possible. They may have an absolute right to be agitated and hateful. They also have the absolute right to hang in there with that hate and agitation until the day they die. It's their choice, and no one can tell them they shouldn't or can't.

HOW TO BE MERCIFUL?

There's a fable told about a captain guiding his ship through an ominous cloudy night. Suddenly from within the murky midst, a light appears dead ahead in the ship's path. The captain grabs his megaphone and with all due authority announces toward the light, "Change your course 10° east!"

From the direction of the light comes a reply, "Change *your* course 10° west!"

The offended captain says, "I'm a navy captain. Change your course, sir!"

Comes a reply, "I'm a seaman, second class. Change *your* course!"

"I'm a battleship, and I'm not changing course!"

One last reply, "I'm a lighthouse. It's your call!"

The undeniable moral: There are always consequences to our choices. What may seem like fidelity to a cause may, in fact, be a deceptive determination undergirded by stubbornness. For a number of proven reasons, such resolute anger can very easily develop into an existence of life-syphoning woundology, a self-identifying victimhood, which is neither peace-giving nor liberating. Such painful ideology and spirituality can easily be passed down from generation to generation within societies or families, movements, or groups, as well as from individual to individual.

All healing, whether physical, mental, or emotional, starts from the inside of a person. In other words, for offended people, the solution, the means, and the way to their peace is not dependent on what happens outside themselves but totally what they choose to transpire within themselves. If we're talking physical wounds, the body forms a protective scab over the injury in order to defend the body against infection. The body can focus on the required internal healing. But if the ill person persists in picking at the bodily sore, s/he not only obstructs honest healing but invites extended infection. The mind and emotions have their own appropriate, protective ideas, and memories which need to be honored if there is any hope of healing. The inner working of our spirituality, in other words our soul's intentions and strivings, are going to be key here one way or the other.

Anyone in pain is, by that simple reality, vulnerable. S/he needs to be doubly alert to others who, in a misguided attempt to show understanding and empathy, would volunteer that "you will have to live with this the rest of your life." Such a forecast can easily turn into a prophecy needing fulfillment. There are too many striking examples of people who have endured unthinkable pain, who have successfully chosen to do what's necessary to move on with their lives to find personal peace and happiness. Depending upon the quality of the wound, outside of some sure miracle, deep hurts are not ordinarily healed or forgiven in a flash and never without God's assistance. So if a person really wants personal peace, that direction needs to be clearly investigated and chosen!

Time Heals: If

Healing, the gaining of interior peace and freedom, is an influx process, maybe even a yes-today-not-yet-tomorrow process. The paramount question is which tug do we allow to predominate? Which one do we nourish more? If authentic peace is operatively sought, then yes, time can

HOW TO BE MERCIFUL?

help to heal all wounds. There simply is no wound that cannot be holistically healed *if,* i.e., on the condition we are willing to surrender even the tiniest drop of a lingering poison of animosity or the corrosive acid of hate, *if,* i.e., whether we are willing to let go and to get on with life, and *if,* i.e., depending upon our willingness to let go and vulnerably welcome the healing and forgiving Lord to free us of any righteous determination. And for clarity here and without any apology for repetition, it must be said without fear of contradiction—there simply is no hope of genuine interior peace and personal freedom without individually chosen and intended pardon of others. The first one to suffer from hate and bitterness is the bitter, hateful, unable or unwilling-to-forgive person him/herself.

Forgiving another does not mean we agree with what happened. Forgiveness doesn't mean we cannot appropriately confront the wrong or the offender. Forgiveness is about what is possible afterwards. Forgiveness is in no sense a weakness, rather forgiveness requires an exceptional strength as becomes evident from the required process and dynamics. Neither does forgiveness necessarily mean or include physical or affective reconciliation, though some types and degrees of forgiveness may, in fact, lead to such. Forgiveness is about attaining one's own freedom and healing. As already mentioned elsewhere, the first one forgiveness sets free and heals is the forgiver. The first one able to "get on with" his/her life is the forgiver. Jesus knew this well:

> Love your enemies, do good to those who
> hate you, bless those who curse you, pray
> for those who abuse you. Do to others as

69

CELEBRATING COMPASSION

you would have them do to you. If you love those who love you, what credit is that to you? For even sinners love those who love them. If you do good to those who do good to you, what credit is that to you? For even sinners do the same. Be merciful, just as your Father is merciful. For the measure you give will be the measure you get back. (Lk 6:27, 31–33, 36, 38b)

In preparation for the Jubilee year of mercy (December 2015–November 2016), Father Carlos Martins, the Roman curate who accompanied the US pilgrimage of the body of St. Maria Goretti, reminded us: "She, of course, is the patroness of mercy." That's because by an already-present grace in her life, even at the age of only eleven, young Maria traversed from the horrific shock of attempted physical trauma and then martyrdom to complete compassionate concern and forgiveness of her offender, Alessandro Serenelli. Already anchored in her youthful soul, it was a forgiving love witnessed to and defined by Jesus. It was precisely her compassion, which God used as an instrument to move Alessandro to solid repentance and personal pursuit of holiness. Underscoring the startling disparity between that compassionate concern of Maria for her offender and lots of present-day reaction to offenses, and in many ways echoing John Paul II, "the pope of mercy," Father Martins cautioned:

We're living in an age where revenge is craved and sought after. The focus is so

HOW TO BE MERCIFUL?

much on standing up for oneself, that for someone who has offended, there is no room for any mercy or compassion upon him or her. To forgive an offender is one way to express mercy that no one is talking about.

Martin Luther King, Jr. said, "Darkness cannot drive out darkness, only light can do that. Hate cannot drive out hate, only love can do that."

Often enough, people do want to forgive and to move on with their lives, but they don't exactly know how. The original hurt, though even of many years ago, may still seem to be as tender and demanding of attention as when it first occurred. They wonder why. Or sometimes, people say they thought they had already forgiven, but because the memory keeps coming back, someone else tells them they really haven't forgiven. Let's look at these phenomena using two images. The first image comes out of eastern Taoism.

One day, the sage gives the disciple an empty sack and a basket of potatoes, and he instructs his student, "Think of all the people who have offended you in the recent past, especially those you can't forgive. Put the name of each offender on a potato and put in the sack."

The disciple comes up with quite a few names, and soon the sack is pretty heavy.

"Now carry the sack wherever you go for a week," says the sage.

At first, carrying the sack isn't too difficult. But after a while, it becomes a real burden, and besides that, it begins to smell terrible. But finally, the week is over, and when the

CELEBRATING COMPASSION

disciple returns, the sage asks if he has learned anything. "Yes, master. When we aren't willing to forgive others, we carry a weight around with us everywhere. And just like these potatoes, that negativity is not only a real burden, but after a while, it stinks. It required so much effort, I decided to forgive everyone who had offended me."

"Great!" says the sage. "Then we can remove all the potatoes... By the way, anybody else offend you within recent days?"

"As a matter fact, yes," replies the disciple.

All at once, he realizes his sack is already getting heavy again, and there will surely be other offenses in coming weeks and months. What did he have to expect for the rest of his life? Would he ever have a really empty sack? So he asks the master, "If we continue like this, wouldn't there always be potatoes in my sack?"

Responds the teacher, "Well, yes, as long as people speak or act against you in some way, you will always have potatoes."

The disciple says, "I can't control what others do. So what control do I have over the burden?"

"I've been waiting for you to ask. The true wisdom of forgiveness is not just the conscious decision to throw away some potatoes. That's just the conventional approach to forgiveness. Figure it out. If the potatoes are angry, hurt feelings, then what is the sack? It's what allows us to save the hurt, angry feelings. It's that guarded space within that allows us to dwell on hurt feelings. Actually, it's our swollen ego, our inflated sense of self-importance!"

"So then how do I not get caught with such un-forgiving feelings?"

"Get rid of the sack!"

Bonfire of Hurt

The second image is that of a large bonfire. To keep a bonfire going, you have to keep feeding it. If you want it to go out, you stop feeding it. No serious academic degree needed here. What people don't recognize is that each time the perturbed memory raises it's agitated attention-demanding head, and they give it time, attention, and energy, they are in reality stoking the fire. Recalling what happened to them, what they should have said or not said, what they should have done or not done, they are energetically—even if unconsciously—turning the smoldering, seething embers over and over. They are providing fresh oxygen and reinvesting into the momentum. The greater the inferno, the longer it's going to burn. The heart beats faster, the blood starts racing again, emotions arise. Imagination can run rampant. The result: people think there's something fresh there.

Let's stay with this bonfire image for a minute. Everyone who's ever seen a bonfire has, in the updraft of heat, seen sparks spontaneously soar into the air. Though the embers may look quite innocent, seemingly insignificant, actually they are another inferno in-the-making. It would be extremely dangerous to deny their existence and danger, thinking they're of no consequence and will take care of themselves. So if we're smart, we pay attention to the reality. We need to decide what to do with those seeming innocent, spontaneous sparks. If we want another fire—fine. We invest in the embers; we blow on them; we

CELEBRATING COMPASSION

give them attention; and we nourish them with additional twigs. But if we really aren't interested in starting another fire, we determine not to further empower them, to extinguish them as quickly as possible; the sooner, the better before they can get beyond our ability to control. The moral: unattended sparks can spread into a raging hellhole! So can unattended wounded emotions. Further, if we're smart, we consciously name them, evaluate their worth and value, and determine what measure of psyche and soul we want to devote to them if any. And again, the sooner, the better.

For wounded persons to set their sights on healing, they need to come to a time when they frankly realize and accept the truth that they cannot change the past or what happened. Further, particularly of wounds inflicted years ago, the mind has had its day, run its course—or should have! They will never have a fresh insight or brand-new idea—they've had them all already. Instead, they are rehashing the same old memories, adversarial emotions, and cantankerous thoughts. None of the present-moment memories or thinking has the ability to suddenly or miraculously alleviate or heal—no more than the time before. It's like beating the same dead drum of memories in the same dead corner. The memories go nowhere positive or hopeful, and they certainly are not freeing. They are not in any sense of the word *life-giving*, but they are life-shaping. Not all memories are worth keeping. Maybe it's time to give them all to God once and for all. Such is not easy. The sting may hang in there—as do evil spirits opposed to forgiveness. But again, "with God, all things are possible" (Mk 10:27).

HOW TO BE MERCIFUL?

Forgiveness and liberating peace do not, cannot, and will not happen by chance. They must become quite deliberate and determined choices. Forgiving mercy needs a sane strategy. This is such an absolute and conditional necessity that when the throbbing memory, negative thinking, or conversation returns, and the suffering individual realizes s/he is back again into the deadbeat corner, rather than continue the frenzied feeding and energizing of the hurt, rather than getting back to the dead drum beating, with and by God's grace s/he immediately opts to surrender the offensive memories to God—maybe again and again, and again. Why? Because God alone is the Savior and Healer. "Come to me, all you who are weary and carrying heavy burdens, and I will give you rest. Take my yoke upon you and learn from me, for I am gentle and humble in heart, and you will find rest for your souls" (Mt 11:28–29). A better and delivering habit is formed.

Mercy and Memory

At times, people have, indeed, already forgiven. But when strong angry emotions surprisingly preempt, for instance, even a prayerful recall, the past chosen compassion can be—at least for the moment—unconsciously reshuffled back into the hurtful maze. So the memory itself needs to be reminded by repeating the choice of pardon. Just because the pained memory resurfaces does not mean sincere and graced forgiveness hasn't already taken place, but it needs consciously to be reaffirmed. Memory needs to be trained. As always, sustained habit is formed by repetition. Genuine and complete forgiving is a birthing process

75

with all the accompanying sting and labor pains. But just like a birthing mother who sees her newborn, the forgiver "no longer remembers the pain" (Jn 16:21) because of her/his new-found peace of soul.

Healing Prayer: A Blessing Prayer

Praying for those who have wounded us is a most powerful medicine fostering personal interior peace. Prayer is the lubricant of spiritual integration. But evidently, it surely cannot be a prayer of retribution—"God, give it to him/her/them!"

There may be some of that wounded attitude at the beginning, and it might—at the beginning—be understandable. But again, that's not peaceful and never can be.

> Finally, all of you have unity of spirit, sympathy, love for one another, a tender heart, and a humble mind. Do not repay evil for evil or abuse for abuse, but on the contrary, repay with a blessing. It is for this that you were called—that you might inherit a blessing. (1 Pt 3:8–9)

Prayer contact with God, even if only feebly in the beginning, helps to move personal injury and suffering into another category. Prayer begins to mobilize alleviation. So healing prayer needs to mature into a blessing prayer: "Lord, free them, him/her. Let them know your love and your peace. May they, too, attain holiness, true happiness

HOW TO BE MERCIFUL?

and eternal life." Such prayer is not only a personally freeing prayer, but it seriously stunts the devil's antics.

No one needs to travel the road of forgiving unaccompanied. Sharing with a trusted confidant would be a distinct advantage. This could be a spouse, a friend, a minister, or a spiritual director. At such times, a good Christian therapist could also be quite a gift. However, therapy—even with a knowledgeable Christian therapist—can do just so much. All guidance ought to lead to genuine personal peace, but the first and unavoidable door to that peace is through active forgiveness. Truth speakers and guides might be able to help a pained person to the very threshold of mercy, but the door to operative forgiveness needs to be opened by the offended person him/herself. Then s/he needs to take the step inside. No proxies, no messengers are admitted or acceptable.

So where find the cajoling strength to cross that threshold of forgiveness? Among several mercy-building supports would be to plan a day or two of prayerful reflection centered on the theme and gift of mercy. Secondly, writing can often be an outstanding instrument of positive insight and movement toward peace. The caution would be not to allow a one-sidedness. In other words, seeing one's own fears or lingering angers expressed in black-and-white can be quite surprising—maybe shocking—as well as informative.

Intended for one's self alone, the writer is free to spell out one's resentments, hurts, or disappointments. But so as not to be slanted by the weight of the burdens, it needs to include one's personal consolations, gifts, positive values, and hopes. Owning one's own goodness may just be the happy grace to push one's self further along the lines of forgiveness. Thirdly, getting acquainted with and being honestly involved in the *Divine Mercy* way of life would be a clear grace. Based on Jesus' own words to St. Faustina, it's a profound spirituality and discipline of asking for and then, in turn, passing on mercy. There simply are no shortcuts. It takes a prepared decision of a disciplined heart, especially to persist in choosing to own and to share Christ's compassion.

Prayers for healing of memories ought to come naturally. Healing of memories does not necessarily mean the memory totally disappears, but that the recall no longer carries with it the pained, self-depleting baggage. That baggage is what we let go of; that's what we choose to forget. We do not forgive because it is easy, but because it's what God has done for us first before asking us to do the same. It's God's mind and heart.

It's so easy to ask God for mercy for ourselves, expecting a loving, prompt, and positive response. It's so easy to take God's mercy for granted. But until we are asked to forgive that someone who has seriously hurt us, we often have little sense or appreciation of the Divine Mercy toward ourselves.

Anyone who really wants to be free of the burden of non-forgiveness needs to begin by looking into one's own life. Am I myself a sinner? Have I ever hurt another by my sins? Do I, too, need forgiveness from anyone? What need I change, let go of in my life, e.g. anger, righteousness, self-pity, impulse to retaliate, to get even, etc., none of which seems to be either life-giving, much less sanctifying?

Any number of people discover that it's much easier to forgive others than self. Let's examine Jesus' witness. There's

HOW TO BE MERCIFUL?

not a single occasion of Jesus encountering a sinner where he shames or condemns, castigates or embarrasses that sinner, neither privately—much less publicly. For instance, on the occasion of a raucous mob wanting to stone an intimidated and frightened adulteress, Jesus calmly challenges the rabble back, "Let him/her without sin cast the first stone." In turn, he doesn't sermonize her but simply—"neither do I condemn you. Go and sin no more" (Jn 8:11). Divine Mercy makes it clear that Jesus relates identically to us when we've sinned. He asks us to treat ourselves the same.

There are two irritants to a genuine self-forgiving process. First is being told, "God forgives you," but the way we are actually treated by society, family, or church community, nevertheless, belies that proclamation. Secondly, there's a conniving stealthy Satan hanging around to sow doubt about God's caring and distrust of any divine mercy.

Self-forgiveness

For the repentant sinner who pines for a valid forgiveness of self, an impatient, hopeful, and reconciling God asks three appropriate questions: (1) Are you genuinely sorry? (2) Are you going to do it again? (3) Have you learned?

Our soul's tranquility is conditioned on how we answer. So when we respond, "Absolutely, I am most heartfully sorry," secondly, "My intentions are never to repeat my wrongful actions," and thirdly, "Without doubt, I'm different, and I'm wiser. With your help, watch my life from this point on!" Then the heart of the good news is that the Lord takes us where we are this day, this moment, not yesterday, not last year, certainly not five or twenty-five years ago. God's eager *abba/amma* mercy takes us at our word, as we do God at God's word.

A 2014 episode of *Blue Bloods*, "Forgive and Forget," asked a most provocative, totally Christian question, "Should a good man be condemned for his worse act or should he be given a second chance?" St. John Paul II knew this exact reality: "We are not the sum of our weaknesses and failures; we are the sum of the Father's love for us and our real capacity to become the image of His Son Jesus" (*World Youth Day* in Toronto, 2002).

Lastly, so as not to lose heart and turn back along what may be a difficult but not impossible journey, a repetitive, loving, reaffirming patience with one's self is a significant requisite.

We learn from the experience of compassion and love that it is ever so much more important to be a giver than a taker in life. However, the truly compassionate person has a willingness "to be taken" by others because s/he knows in truth that if s/he gives from a motive of love, s/he is never really "taken." Though the gaining of personal joy and peace is a significant reason for ministering to another our forgiveness, the rock-bottom reason for forgiving others is after all godliness within, otherwise known as holiness.

The gospel is not predominantly about the innocent being saved, as about sinners who are converted in and through their sorrow and seek forgiveness! In other words, Jesus didn't come to save the already saved—though they, too, are saved only by his grace—but the "lost sheep, the lost coin, the lost son," i.e., those who've made mistakes! Salvation's pristine motive being mercy, it begins and ends with compassion. "Forgiveness demonstrates the presence

HOW TO BE MERCIFUL?

in the world of the love, which is more powerful than sin" (St. John Paul II, *Rich in Mercy*, n. 14). Pope Francis reflects with us upon "the God who manifests his power above all by forgiveness and mercy" (*Prayer for the Jubilee Year of Mercy*). As we choose forgiveness, we ourselves become the concrete presence and force for viable godliness in our pilgrim world.

Dear St. Maria Goretti,
Patroness of Mercy,
your heart was so full of mercy,
that you gladly forgave your assassin,
and prayed that he might be saved;
Intercede for me before the Lord,
Whom you now behold face-to-face.
Ask him to pour his grace into my soul
so that I may always be ready to imitate Jesus as you did.
I choose you as my friend this day
and I ask you to accompany me my whole life long.
In honor of the Most Holy Name of Jesus,
and in imitation of your example,
I forgive all who have ever hurt me
or who desired my suffering,
and I ask pardon of all against whom I have sinned.
Through Christ our Lord.
Amen.

(From a holy card accompanying St. Maria Goretti's body as it toured the United States during the Jubilee Year of Mercy.)

6

Rethinking "Unforgivable" Pain

Have you ever worked on a thousand-piece picture puzzle depicting a beautiful wintry scene? You set out an appropriately sized table to accommodate the dimensions of the puzzle. You place the top of the box, which portrays the snowy landscape, in front of you so you know what the finished product is supposed to look like. Then you turn all the pieces color side up. And with patience and determination and lots of hope, you begin. It helps to establish the outside frame early. You look for the pieces with a straight edge. There's a back and forth, thinking this piece fits. You move from one area of the scene to build another. It doesn't take long to realize you make a lot of mistaken assumptions. Certain pieces you judged would be the exact ones to fit, don't. You feel rewarded when they do. So it's a try and try again that's needed. By design, all puzzles are intended to challenge us, as well as to award us an accolade of accomplishment when we have, indeed, completed them.

Life's Puzzle

Now suppose you had a truly nondescript puzzle before you of an undetermined number of pieces, colors, and contours. You dump all the pieces on the table, but they have to remain in the position they fell—no turning over for colors. There's no scene on the top of the box but only general hints about what the scene is supposed to look like when finished. Adding to the brainteaser is a further dilemma, namely there are extra pieces. Some are look-alikes, some exact duplicates, and some don't even belong to the puzzle. Other people can enter the room where you're working. Some will not only tell you what piece ought to go where, but if you're not watching, they may move or remove a piece. You have no idea how large the actual puzzle is eventually going to be. No ordinary puzzle. The bewildering challenge is to figure out the mystery in all its complexities.

There are unavoidable imperfections, crosses, woundedness, and a dying and death in everyone's life. They are co-natural to the human condition. They are dead center integral to the unpredictable puzzle of life. But by vocation, their challenge is heightened and intensified in a Christian's life as a pilgrim being ushered into holiness. How else could it be? How else should it be? Jesus was very upfront: "If any want to become my followers, let them deny themselves and take up their cross and follow me" (Mt 16:24). Consequently, why are we so unprepared, surprised, and often disgruntled when the paschal mystery enters our lives?

What is this so-called "paschal mystery" anyway? What's its purpose? How does it fit into the puzzle of life?

The Paschal Piece

The term "paschal" derives from the Latin *pascha* meaning "feast of Passover." It takes on its Christian connotation from Jesus celebrating his "Last Supper" probably on the preparation day for the Jewish festivity of Passover. But the innate meaning of "paschal lamb" has a concomitant connotation of vicarious suffering, i.e., taking on the pain of another for, and in the place of the other. In other words, there's a standing in for, a bleeding in place of another, if you would, precisely to save the other from having to bleed. There's a willingness to pay the debt of another at one's own personal cost. The paschal mystery is called "mystery" with good reason. A major part of that mystery arises with the bewildering question: "Why would anyone even want to do that?" The first Old Testament paschal lamb was a stand-in for the chosen people. Its blood, sprinkled on the doorposts of faithful Jewish homes, alerted the "angel of death" that this family adamantly chose to belong to the one true God. Christianity claims Jesus as the Paschal Lamb of all time.

In his informative book on masculine spirituality, *Wildmen, Warriors, and Kings*, the late Jesuit, Patrick M. Arnold, wrote that unless men choose to be more than mere passive observers of life, they must seriously prepare to live with what he refers to as *agonia*. Why? Because agony/suffering, whether of a male or female, is one of the main thrust engines of human growth and maturing. Our personal ability to assess suffering and pain is at the heart of deciphering the puzzle of life.

The English word *agony* is based on the Greek term *agon*. Having some sense of what Jesus' "agony in the garden" meant is a good tip-off for its full meaning. It not only denotes the deep, gut-wrenching pressures involved in any serious conflict, be it physical or emotional, but looks for some redeeming purpose underlying the pain. It doesn't want the contest to be in vain. *Agon* hopes for eventual total alleviation, i.e., for more than the proverbial "light at the end of the tunnel." Rather, due to the burdensome investment, it yearns for a significant, informing light that endures beyond the contest and the tunnel. It looks for some redeeming value to the pain at hand. However, permeating the contest is a decision to be value-true to self.

Rites of Passage Contribution

In ages past in certain cultures, a fledgling but maturing male was wisely prepared to engage the puzzle of life. Under the solicitous eyes of experienced elders (i.e., teachers, wise men, or *shamans*) at a carefully chosen time, the initiate(s) was taken away from the mother to a secluded sacred place. These "initiation rites" had the integral teaching components of humiliation and pain.

Male initiation rites are a confirmed setting for unpacking the hidden lessons of pain and humiliation. However, let's not miss the reality that women, by the very virtue of being women, have the pain of menstrual cycles and labor pains—their own "rites of passage" based on nature's "coming of age." They, too, have their elders to guide.

The purposes of any "rites of passage," whether for males or females, were several.

First of all, they were to awaken within the inexperienced youth an affirming consciousness of a hidden, inner wo/man, i.e., the formidable, wondrous and mysterious strength yet untapped. It's like the strength and vibrancy of a young wild stallion. To be safe, useful, and at its best potential, its strength and vibrancy need channeling through the skilled schooling of bridle and bit. Initiation rites are about teaching the wise use of the bridle and bit called self-knowledge and self-control.

The School of Humility and Pain

Secondly, the rites were to make undeniably evident that pain and humiliation have the potential to teach more than do the pleasures of life. Pain grabs our attention sooner. Humility accents our poverty of not having all the answers to life's challenges. Pain lingers and processes itself in the gut of life. Reacting, we can endlessly confront pain by just cursing the dark, or we can dare ourselves to respectfully embrace the pain in order to learn from it a distinct wisdom, i.e., garnering something very special not only about life but for life. But depending upon one's attitude, the wounded person may have to be quite patient to reap the veiled gift, the "treasure buried in the field" of suffering.

Thirdly, the arduous rites demonstrate that the path to maturity is, indeed, an ongoing, if not at times, a very drawn-out journey. It is a passage never traveled quickly nor in exact straight lines, but more often through trial and error. As the sign reads: "Wisdom is learned from experience. Experience is learned from mistakes." After all, when

RETHINKING "UNFORGIVABLE" PAIN

exactly does any one of us reach a stage of maturity beyond which there is nothing more to learn and to appropriate? There are no thirty-day wonders here. The initiating ordeal gives but a vision, sets a direction, and fosters hope. Having persevered this time, the initiate can endure again, hopefully in a wiser way. Part of that learned wisdom is the realization that the elders were not merely helpful but indispensable in getting through the test.

Fourthly, the initiate is not called to this taxing rite of passage for the sake of the ritual itself, e.g., like a college or military hazing, nor even or exclusively for the sake of the individual alone, rather there's an inherent social learning aspect of the rite. The initiate is summoned to the contest, ultimately for the sake of owning responsibilities toward others, toward the common good. What s/he was asked to undergo is but a foretaste of what s/he may have to withstand for the benefit of others, e.g., family, friends, neighbors, and/or the larger community. The point being made here is, that at times, the common good may well supersede an individual's personal benefit, all part of the larger puzzle.

Evidently, there are countless possible degrees of personal pain. But initiation rites are about more than merely stubbing one's toe. Rather the attention-demanding experience has an unmistakable sense of being broken, of being defeated. There's a haunting tone of disaster, of a tumbling down from a decent social status into humbling "kitchen work" or to "the road of ashes." Because it definitely connotes formidable serious hurt, if one desires both wisdom and healing, it's going to demand overt concentration.

No doubt, being willing to learn from a particular hurt would have to be at the heart of any healing. Naturally enough, the initial response to any pain is doing all in our power to stop it, to decidedly run from it, and to avoid it in the future if at all possible. Yet not surprisingly, some pain is already known about, even chosen beforehand. That's exactly what occurs when we are willing to endure a seriously taxing discomfort as a necessary means to an end, a prize, e.g. training for a race, losing weight, studying for the exam, or preparing for surgery. Why not expect and wisely prepare for it within the journey to holiness?

All pain gathers and stores information, from the physical headache or toe stubbing, to the ache of someone deeply wounding our hearts. As such, while not chosen in or for itself, pain becomes an apt meaningful occasion and condition of learning. What's wrong? What's the cause of my pain? What can I do about it? Again, while the natural temptation is to sidestep pain, in doing so, we squander any inherent, life-giving lesson of life and soul. The greater the pain, the more meaningful the resultant, potential lessons for life. It's all "potential" because it's going to depend on how vulnerable we are to the lesson being offered.

Descending into Pain

In his book, *Iron John*, Robert Bly uses a Greek word we're not familiar with, namely *katabasis*. Translated, it means "a descending, a going down and into" something. But this "going down and into" is not, for instance, just like a quick curious dipping of one's foot into the pool of life to discover its temperature. Rather it's an unconditional

RETHINKING "UNFORGIVABLE" PAIN

plunge, a stark, skinny-dipping immersion into the pool of life in search of its secluded lessons.

The cross is part of anyone's pool of life. But why be willing to endure suffering at all? Not only is part of the response found in sharing in the cross of Jesus, but suffering often carries within it hidden lessons. The Christian truth is: the deeper the suffering, the more precious its discoverable value. But in the face of especially serious hurt, the temptation is to stay on the surface rather than to go down and into it. We'd rather deal with what we think we can control. We may also have accompanying apprehensions. For instance, as an individual, I may not be open to learn more about life, especially about *my* life! There may be lessons I'm not ready nor willing to engage. But it's just such wisdom discovered only down in the winepress of suffering and stress, which is the very goal and prize of *katabasis*!

Emptying Self of Self

Following a rather dramatic conversion, St. Paul comes to know the experience of being interiorly dismantled from the inside out. Then because he knows the reality so well, he is able to recognize the identical dynamic in Jesus' life. Paul describes it: "Though he was in the form of God, (he) did not regard equality with God as something to be exploited, but *emptied himself*, taking on the form of a slave, being born in human likeness. And being found in human form, he *humbled himself* and became obedient to the point of death—even death on a cross" (Phil 2: 6–8). The Greek word Paul used to depict Jesus' "emptying himself, humbling himself" was *kenosis*. It's the chastening, denuding

89

CELEBRATING COMPASSION

process of "emptying, purging one's self of self." The motive behind the "emptying/purging one's self of self" is beautifully epitomized in "I must decrease." Why? "So Christ can increase" (Jn 3:30). It's from just a descent (*katabasis*) into our personal suffering and woundedness that we discover certain life-giving values and liberating truths, which until now lay hidden, and hence, unexamined in the shadowy recesses of "unforgivable pain."

There are two possible responses to personal wounds and suffering. One response to pain is to react impetuously out of habit and instinct rather than choosing a measured, self-liberating response. Like an as-yet-untested adolescent dismissing the whole point of "rites of passage," we give the possibility of learning from pain and pressure the old stiff arm. We adamantly refuse to accept, much less purposefully going down into the school of hurt to learn anything. On top of that, we defensively deny any urgency to process our wounds. "I'm doing fine!" We dig in our heels, and at all costs, shun any healthy, personal self-examination. We consciously evade answering: "Who am I becoming by the way I'm handling this pain?" However, being unable or unwilling to opt for personally-alleviating forgiveness of others—and surely even of self at times—merely assists one's own sulking toward a draining depression and restlessness. The solving of life's puzzle is at least temporarily suspended.

The second option of dealing with pain alone offers hope and a glimmer of light at the end of what is at times a very long tunnel.

There is a radical difference between being hurt and the mystery referred to here as "paschality." Paschality calls

RETHINKING "UNFORGIVABLE" PAIN

us to the humbling truth, acceptance, and embracing of the wound—that "self-emptying of self"—in order to sound out the screaming hurt in its depths for any sage messages. It's getting "the self" out of the way, i.e., one's biases, presumptions, ignorance, and one's importance! That's humbling! But note well. It's humility which is the actual promising doorway to the hidden inner sanctums of wisdom. Don't forget, "sanctum" refers to "holy." Humility assists us to address the questions: "Why me? How can this be happening? Why do I deserve this?"

By its nature, humility disarms us of our usual defenses. Our covert vulnerabilities, our unadmitted inabilities, as well as our ill-formed prejudices rise to full consciousness—if not at times, to full public gawking. And we stand psychologically, emotionally, and spiritually exposed. We're mortified! Again, that's humbling! As a result of that interior stripping off and away, our souls become more porous; our hearts more receptive. God has us exactly where God wants us: "In your weakness [humility] is my strength" (2 Cor 12:9). Appropriately, Frances de Sales taught: "There is no other wisdom except that which comes from the Holy Spirit, and that wisdom is given only to the humble." Scripture chimes in: "For gold is tried in fire and chosen ones in the furnace of humiliation" (Eccl 2:5).

There is no gaining of wisdom possible unless and until one comes to an absolutely naked descent into and with the unadorned pain. Such vulnerability is indispensable. It's an indisputable condition to sit in face-to-face dialogue with it. Only then can we openly embrace our cross and learn from it the tough lessons it has to teach—just like the innocent as yet inexperienced initiates.

CELEBRATING COMPASSION

Then what's needed is the courage to ask: "What's the lesson here? What personally-honing wisdom is contained herein? How does God want me to use this?" It cannot be a wisdom-gaining occurrence until the aching pilgrim chooses to be vulnerable enough to learn from the experience of grief and surrenders. It cannot be a wisdom-forming event until the wounded person chooses *kenosis*, that buck naked emptying of self. Only then in that unprotected, seemingly demeaning vulnerability is it possible to discover a new and even stronger life, a converted and improved life, if not also a joyful, free, and peaceful life. It's just such a wisdom-birthing process that gives meaning to the phrase: "the womb of the wound."

O Happy Fault

When we are youngsters growing up, we don't yet have the capacity to judge the worth and value of parental discipline. Ordinarily, we think it to be unfair, ill-placed, and ill-advised. It's only as we ourselves mature and have to deal with our own choices and behavior that we get the hindsight into the grace and blessings of what was appropriate discipline. Sure, we can stubbornly hamper and stunt pain's teaching wisdom. But why impede a second look?

There might even come the startling insight that what I personally learned from the debilitating wound was actually a deep, unexpected grace. It might come in a startling awareness: "Look how that turned out!" It's like original sin is referred to at the Easter vigil as a *felix culpa*, i.e., "a happy fault," due to a consequential incarnation of the Son of God. It's the graced mindfulness that the personal benefit

RETHINKING "UNFORGIVABLE" PAIN

of my own consternating hurt has far outweighed its original pain. For example, what's the courage I learned in the face of hardship? What's the ability I gained to process pain and disagreement? What's the personal endurance I cultivated? What have I learned about human relationships, about how to treat others?" One's prayer might well wind up being, "Thank you, Jesus, for accompanying me on my own way of Gethsemane and the cross and bringing me to resurrection." Memory can be very life-giving. It's a reconciling realization that what was, was; what is, is; what will be, may well be—but due to my new-found wisdom, it's not inevitable.

Ascending from Pain

This awareness is more than just an important hope-filled piece to the puzzle of life, rather it gives direction and purpose to tying the whole puzzle together. This tedious reaping of wisdom directly from within pain, this arising out of and away from the angers and stagnant judgments of life, is the corresponding updraft, the counterpoint to *katabasis-kenosis* called *anabasis*. It is the liberating "ascending," an emergence found in the wisdom of forgiving another. The awkward work and throb of forgiving is accomplished in the company of Another and passed on to our higher power. Possible? "My grace is sufficient for you; my power is at its best in weakness" (2 Cor 12:7–10). The Lord is surely willing to heal us, but we need to do our part.

"My brothers and sisters, whenever you face trials of any kind, consider it nothing but joy, because you know that the testing of your faith produces endurance; and let

CELEBRATING COMPASSION

endurance have its full effects, so that you may be mature and complete, lacking in nothing" (Jas 1:2–4).

Following some quite deep personal anguish in his life, Henri Nouwen taught us about personal *anabasis*: "When we become aware that we do not have to escape our pains, but that we can mobilize them into a common search for life, those very pains are transformed from expressions of despair into signs of hope" (*Wounded Healers*).

Shared within the identical context is another very inspiring reflection written by Sister Sue Mosteller, CSJ— for many years, director of Henri Nouwen Literary Center and also director of L'Arche, following Jean Vanier as international coordinator:

> When we know the pain of abandonment, loss, or rejection; there is hope for us as well.
>
> We need patience and a deep respect for the time it takes to grieve our real losses and to own them as our own.
>
> We need lots of time and support to give up our expectation that someone can erase or change what actually happened that wounded us.
>
> We need to share and ask for support in our network of friends, of family, church, or community where people will not be scandalized when they hear that our once cherished relationships are complicated, difficult, less than perfect, or gone altogether.

RETHINKING "UNFORGIVABLE" PAIN

And gradually, when the time is right, we need encouragement to step through and beyond our grief into new and renewed relationships of trust, where we once again recover our ability to care for others and our sense of humor. (Weavings XIII, September/October 1998)

Ultimately, only faith and trust in Jesus' redeeming passion and death can help to transform any human suffering into a paschal event. "Through your faith, God's power will guard you…even though you may for a short time have to bear being plagued by all sorts of trials" (1 Pet. 1:6–9).

7

Parameters of Divine Mercy

Unqualified Divine Mercy

As Divine Mercy, Jesus professes undying, eager love and fidelity, an impatient willingness and readiness to forgive each and every sinner. As a matter of fact, he pointedly stipulates that it is precisely *as* sinner and *because* we are sinners that we have a divinely bequeathed, rightful claim on his inexhaustible compassion. God's crystal-clear preference is a bountiful mercy which tempers justice. It is we humans who impose limitations. So Jesus comes as Divine Mercy, and through Faustina talks in terms anyone can understand:

> The greater the sinner, the greater the right s/he has to my mercy. (*Diary*, n. 723)
> Know that my heart is mercy itself. From this sea of mercy, grace flows out upon the whole world. No soul that has

PARAMETERS OF DIVINE MERCY

approached me has ever gone away uncon-
soled. (*Diary*, n. 1777)

Tell the whole world of my great
mercy... My heart rejoices in the title of
mercy. (*Diary*, n. 300)

Proclaim that mercy is the greatest
attribute of God. All the works of my hands
are crowned with mercy. (*Diary*, n. 301)

The flames of mercy are burning
me—clamoring to be spent. (*Diary*, n. 50
and 177)

Encourage souls to place great trust in
my fathomless mercy. Let the weak sinful
soul have no fear to approach me, for even
if it had more sins than there are grains of
sand in the world, all would be drowned
in the unmeasurable depths of my mercy.
(*Diary*, n. 1059)

I cannot punish even the greatest sinner if he makes an appeal to my compassion... I justify him in my unfathomable
and inscrutable mercy. Write: before I
come as a just Judge, I first open wide the
door of my mercy. (*Diary*, n. 1146)

The greater the misery of the soul,
the greater its right to my mercy...no one
have I excluded! (*Diary*, n. 1182)

I am mercy itself. (*Diary*, n. 1739)

Note well. Faustina never qualified any of Divine
Mercy's words with the slightest implied caution, e.g.,

"unless s/he did 'this or that;' unless s/he's a politician, a judge, or a family member; unless s/he's a teacher; unless he's a priest or bishop!" Rather as we've just read, it's with decisive emphasis Jesus clearly, unapologetically teaches: "No one have I excluded!" This is one of the very first unlimited parameters confirmed by Divine Mercy.

Creature "I" and Divine Mercy

Secondly, the divine mercy mantra, "Jesus, I trust you," is all about unwavering reliance on every word Jesus shared with Faustina. But when you think about it, just who is the "I" before the burning bush of God's mercy? Just to utter these words, *Jesus, I trust you*, has to suggest at least a tone of human arrogance. Who am *I* as creature—even worse, as sinner—to have the gall to say, "*I* trust *you, God?*" But it's Jesus who starts it all! He's the one giving the possibility and impetus to my trusting. "Jesus, I trust you" means "I am soulfully, irreversibly convinced of your loving intentions and goodness toward me. I trust you, i.e., that you want my eternal happiness as the first and ultimate criteria of why you not only created me in the first place, but of why you stay doggedly concerned and present in my life, even my weak and sinful life." It's God's unwavering *modus operandi*. The invitation to say, "Jesus, I trust you," is a luring "come on" to get us into conversation with him. It sounds so innocent, so welcoming. First, we get hooked and then need to reflect upon what we've been praying. Trust is a virtuous quality born of an experience of an incoming love of another's dependable, unwavering benevolence and concern. The affirmation, "I trust you," is one of those realities

PARAMETERS OF DIVINE MERCY

similar to "I love you." Even if it's not yet a perfect love, not yet a perfect trust, it will grow and mature in meaning the more we mean it when we say it.

When you put all Divine Mercy's teachings together side-by-side, it almost comes across as too much to take in, too much to believe, and too good to be true. As Jesus put it himself: "Souls just don't want to believe in my goodness" (*Diary*, n. 177). But as has been already reflected upon elsewhere in these reflections, if we can't or won't take God at God's word, then what or who else becomes the basis of our truth, trust, and hope in place of God?

Additionally, the words and promises of Divine Mercy are so hope-filled and consoling, so uplifting that unless prayerfully and vulnerably reflected upon, they can lend themselves to being taken advantage of and exaggerated. At times, Divine Mercy may well feel like saying, "Wait! I never promised that!" So there's an inherent need for Divine Mercy's teachings to be properly nuanced by sound spiritual wisdom. For instance, Divine Mercy states:

> These souls have a right of priority to my compassionate heart, they have first access to my mercy. Tell them that no soul that has called upon My mercy has been disappointed or brought to shame. I delight particularly in a soul which has placed its trust in my goodness. (*Diary*, n. 1541)
>
> I will deny nothing to any soul whom you will bring to the fount of my mercy. (*Diary*, n. 1209)

CELEBRATING COMPASSION

It pleases me to grant everything they ask of me by saying the chaplet. (*Diary*, n. 1541)

Through the chaplet you will obtain everything, if what you ask for is compatible with my will. (*Diary*, n. 1731)

Let's look at these individually.

"These souls have *a right of priority* to my compassionate heart, they have *first access* to my mercy. Tell them *no soul* that has called upon my mercy has been disappointed or brought to shame." (*Italics* added for emphasis.) But anyone, with even a modicum of personal experience praying for personal mercy, knows that this just isn't always the graced result of even our most fervent prayers to Divine Mercy, i.e., that everything turns out immediately and exactly the way and to the degree we'd prefer. Neither is it the hard-proven reality of life that there is never any dark night of lingering physical or mental illness nor within other spheres of pain, e.g., personal and/or public humiliation. So questioning naturally arises. "What's up here? I've been in this mercy line forever! What's this *right of priority* and *first access* all about anyway? I trusted, so how come the Lord allegedly doesn't come through?" Is that even a possibility? Maybe a partial answer is that I've misinterpreted what he seems to be promising. Maybe I've embellished his words to fit my needful version of life. What is the Lord promising exactly? Perhaps the Lord is humbly investigating whether I can continue to trust him, even though there are lingering disappointments in my biased opinion.

PARAMETERS OF DIVINE MERCY

Giving Faustina directions for praying the Divine Mercy novena, Jesus says, "I will deny *nothing* to *any soul* whom you will bring to the fount of my mercy" (*Diary*, n. 1209). But to what does that "nothing" refer? It sure doesn't mean he'll give everything every time we ask, no matter for what we're asking. Rather there's a focus to what he promises not to deny. What he promises never to deny are two distinct graces. Both are virtues, which, of course, he never denies. First, vital for any change of heart on our part is the grace of sorrow for our sins and resolve not to repeat them. The second grace is to be willing to forgive others no matter how difficult. So the "nothing" denied has to do with all the graces needed for our soul's purging transformation, and consequently for fortified lasting soul peace.

Divine Mercy's Compatibility

Later, Jesus adds in, "It pleases me to grant *everything* they ask of me by saying the chaplet" (*Diary*, n. 1541). But then there's a qualified fine print repeat: "Through the chaplet, you will obtain *everything if* what you ask for *is compatible* with my will" (*Diary*, n. 1731). To a wayfaring pilgrim, that's a very attractive and repetitious promise. The natural and great temptation is to pick up on the "to grant *everything*" and "you will obtain *everything*" because these promises seem so all-embracive and filled with hope. At first glance, they fit in so very well with the entire Divine Mercy pledge. However, when not *everything* turns out the way I'd like *everything*, the accompanying temptation is to say, "Well, Jesus, why should I continue to pray and trust you? You didn't keep your word!" Yet again, that can't be

101

true! So I'm called to question my own preferred understanding of what he said. The key comes in the qualifying remaining words of the repeated pledge, namely "if what you ask for is compatible with my will." There's three discerning words here.

First, the "if" is not an incidental qualifier! It is rather an indicator of dependency, i.e., "on the condition that" such and such is a reality. Secondly, the word *compatible* means "agreeable, in tune with, consistent with." Experience may teach that not *everything* we pray for is, in fact, always harmonious with God's own ideas and plans. Neither does *everything* God wills for us begin or finish within our own limited calendar schedule. When things aren't going our way, God is often inviting us to a deeper trust of that divine promise, "I know the plans I have in mind for you, plans for peace and not disaster, reserving a future full of hope for you so that when you seek me, I will let you find me" [and listen up now] "when you seek me with all your heart" (Jer 29:12–14). Not only is the "when" just as conditional as the "if" but so is the "all." It means an all-embracive totality and comprehensiveness of "mind, heart, soul, and strength" (Mk 12:30). Of course, it's often easier to love a God we don't have to deal with on a physical level. That's why God added the test about loving our neighbor, who we can see and have to deal with day in and day out as evidence of a firm, Godlike love within ourselves. This "when you seek me with all your heart" is not only an integral condition, it is an essential prerequisite for holiness and union with the divine.

When we've done our best and honestly trusted God and then events still don't turn out at all the way we hoped for and envisioned, it becomes a salient occasion for the

PARAMETERS OF DIVINE MERCY

devil to raise his prompting head to suggest that we not place so much confidence in God after all. But taking a breath and a step back, and making it a point to rummage through our own depleting disappointment, we may well discover that a major part of the felt disparity is because we've been trying to control and manage God's mercy so that it turns out fulfilling our own finely-honed notion of desire and peace. But as significant and precious as we may hold our own personal peace to be, is it the most important for God, i.e., that we have next-to-perfect peace now, i.e., immediately? Is there perhaps a deeper question God is asking us?

For instance, it's so easy to say, "Jesus, I trust you," when things are going well. It's quite another to say, "Jesus, I trust you," and mean it when things are all vastly disheveled in life, when we feel in a free fall of adversity, when we don't have a clue about where God is or what God is doing. Then the inner churnings of trust call for a deeper double-edged confidence, namely and first: "Lord, I trust you still care and are with me." Secondly: "I trust you know what you're doing!" That we could even so respond is, indeed, already a profound grace of God's mercy. And it's right where God wants us. After all, as God has encouraged us, "My grace is sufficient for you. My power is made perfect in [your] weakness" (2 Cor 12:9). In other words, it's precisely when we're down that we're not so feisty and ready to fight God. For instance, it's been noted, most people in a hospital bed have time for God! A person who visited a hospice every Saturday said, "No one rebelled about dying."

The interior dynamics of trust are very similar to an active faith. We say we believe in things when, in reality, we

103

CELEBRATING COMPASSION

haven't/can't see or weigh them out in actuality. Lacking a verifiable test tube measurement, we have to make a deliberate choice to believe in those unseen realities. Though there may be only limited indicators, there's something else. Maybe even most of the reality is still unseen, and to that extent unknown, but it still makes good convincing sense to believe. St. Paul expressed this so well: "Now faith is the assurance of things hoped for, the conviction of things not seen" (Heb 11:1). The mind, not being fully satisfied, under God's grace is invited to make an act of faith. This is about making a choice, hence, involves the will. I choose to believe because I accept the honesty and goodness of the one who told me. Faith already involves trust. We choose to rely on someone else's consistent truth and honesty, his/her word and promise. We decide to rely on what s/he says when s/he promises to be good, to care for us, and to keep his/her word, even though the ultimate outcome is unforeseen, i.e., unknown to us. The less personal control we are able to invest—the greater quality of trust is demanded.

As we've seen, one arm of Mercy is definitely extended to embrace the sinner. Thank God, because the truth is, we are all sinners! "If you, O Lord, mark iniquities, who could stand?" (Ps 130:3). But an evident second parameter for God's compassion is the heartfelt plea for mercy in the face of life's crosses.

When dealing with the crosses of life, we need to remember and to trust two truths. First, God is always with us, is always on our side. To trust in Divine Mercy, while in the forbidding shadows of a dark night, is not possible without God's help. Secondly and understandably, dark nights are always going to be vocation-appropriate, i.e.,

PARAMETERS OF DIVINE MERCY

God purifies married people as married people, singles as singles, parents as parents, priests and consecrated religious as priests and consecrated religious, and so forth.

Any number of saints are portrayed as eagerly seeking out the cross, any cross—the bigger and heavier, the better. They were trying to prove their love for and union with the crucified Lord. Such are most special graces. Not all of us are called by God to the identical depth of imitation of Christ. For the rest of us, our crosses come out of the facticity of life. It's for that reason, every person has to decide how to address these crosses. Only a person of faith can name them. Only a person of faith can peer into them and discover their purpose. Only a person of faith can see and hope for what is beyond the pain. Pain cajoles us to prioritize our values, and to recommit to them.

Crosses can have various sizes, weights, and shapes. For instance, when our tranquil agenda for body, mind, or emotions is violently disturbed, that's a cross. When our financial responsibilities become too burdensome to meet, we can feel the weight of a cross. Others, withholding their forgiving mercy toward us, provide us a daily "way of the cross." When relational ties become venomous and strangling, we feel the cross of betrayal. When the cavernous sink hole of others' suspicion demeans our own self-esteem, we know the cross of rejection. A pagan, or merely secularistic cross has nothing to offer beyond the pain. The cross of Christ alone emits hope. In the shadow of a Christ-cross, God is present quietly holding a sacred breath, hoping we come to some awareness that this uninvited bout is deliberately allowed. Hence, it has a divine purpose. God alone can change our crosses and trials into seeds of life and even

CELEBRATING COMPASSION

joy. "Where there is doubt, faith; where there is despair, hope" (St. Francis).

God's hesitancy indicates there's some critical lesson of life still to be learned. There's some central wisdom of soul yet lying dormant waiting for a firm grasping. There's a deeper, sacred intimacy to which we are being invited. It's a "spiritual rites of passage." We are being cleverly ushered to a place of discomfort we'd never willingly choose for ourselves. But it's a purifying transformation which can be captured only from within the personally unmanageable ache of the dark night. "I will refine your dross in the furnace, removing all your alloy" (Is 1:21–27).

How quick we learn we are not in control. How undeniable our utter dependency and pilgrim poverty. But the unresolved dark night is but an occasion, a beckoning, an opportunity, and a pointing. The lingering cross starkly indicates the Divine Artisan is still at work, not yet finished with us. Pain, crisis, and suffering are the germinating wherewithal of dark nights, true. But they are, at the same time, the transforming wherewithal of holy nights.

Divine Mercy and Lingering Crosses

Divine Mercy isn't necessarily the alleviating of the cross in one's life but the grace of willingness to shoulder it. Remember the Father Flanagan's poster for *Boys' Town*? It was one young boy carrying his still younger brother on his back and saying, "He ain't heavy. He's my brother." In other words, love transforms the weight and burden; love provides a reason to shoulder the load. In the same measure, while not necessarily totally mitigating our dark

PARAMETERS OF DIVINE MERCY

nights, mercy is an accompanying grace to endure, to learn from, and to be divinized through them. In relation to dying, mercy is surely not that we won't die, e.g., as some evident sign of God's mercy, but that we die a peaceful, going-home death.

The unavoidable suffering involved in the dark nights is imaged quite well in the drama of human birthing, no matter the procedure but especially if it's a natural birthing. There is no way to avoid the connatural pain of delivery completely. But it's only after the infant gift is seen and held that the long-awaited prize transforms the meaning of the pain. "As gold is tried by fire" (Sirach 2:4), i.e., the consuming, separating out, and purifying fire is the inherent price.

God's purpose, beyond the birthing of dark nights, also involves a steep cost. From deep within the recesses of this taxing trial, God is whispering:

> I am not only with you, I am within you, bearing with you every throbbing pain. I sustain you, giving you every support-ive grace needed to endure and to get through this trial. You couldn't possibly do so without my merciful presence. It's decisively my 'now-mercy' which sustains you, in turn, leading you to a still deeper mercy experienced in my undeserved inti-macy and love. I will never tax you beyond the bolstering strength I am conveying to accompany and support you.

CELEBRATING COMPASSION

Teilhard de Chardin propounded: "When and whatever we suffer, we suffer Christ, and Christ suffers in us. We suffer together." In other words, Christ weeps when we weep. Christ too shares our sleepless nights.

But what happens most often at the initial commencement of dark nights is that our anguished cry for mercy is understandably centered on our "now-pain." Still uninitiated, inexperienced, we'd prefer total and immediate alleviation. But remember, "'For my thoughts are not your thoughts, nor are your ways my ways,' says the Lord" (Is 55:8). In other words, God isn't bound up or limited by human logic or reasonableness.

While even the most fervent prayer may not amend God's mind or plan—as it didn't for Jesus in Gethsemane—it does by nature move and strengthen us toward the identical: "Thy will be done." But it turns out, "Thy will be done" is not a once-and-for-all pledge of life. It surely wasn't for our Blessed Mother, as neither for thousands of itinerant pilgrims across the ages. And so develops our mantra: "Thy will be done. Jesus, I trust you." Our own biased vision is naturally and always a short-term vision encapsulating "the here and now." However, we need rather to take a long-term perspective of mercy through God's eyes. While not oblivious to our "here-and-now" trials, God's visionary hope and interest focus rather on our journey's summation. It's like planting a seed. There's a hope-filled vision. There are plans set in motion. There's an invested patient trusting in a germinating of eventual fruit. It demands a patient waiting.

When we come to spiritual genesis, God is the hopeful visionary and the patient sower. First of all, we need to claim God's active inseminating grace of endurance which

PARAMETERS OF DIVINE MERCY

sustains us. Secondly, we need to reach out to the engaging pain. It's a birthing drama of deeper divine intimacy. Throughout this tedious test, not unexpectedly, our anxious, hovering, probing God impatiently waits to know: "Now do you still trust me and my mercy? Do you still trust that I know what I'm doing?"

It takes unmistakable grace to see God's hushed presence within the murkiness of a dark night. But how else could it be? By who else's efforts could it even be possible to do? We have to admit our poverty, our ignorance in the face of the mystery we are staring in the face. Lacking that humble admission, we'll never discover the presence and plan of God veiled in our dark nights. Understandably, of and by themselves, the events will remain obscure without the slightest potential to become sacred nights. Pain as pain is useless, unless it's examined to discover what it's telling us. Only then can pain become a teacher. In the school of dark nights, this is the more tedious, demanding, if not honestly distasteful soul work. But it's worth it! Why? Because this is precisely where the Lord is silently, diligently instigating.

Unless we pause and contemplate an innocent Jesus in his own passion and death—a passion and death he absolutely never personally deserved but accepted upon his own shoulders in order to open eternal life to us—our own suffering might easily appear to be unfair. But what Jesus does is to give us the perfect example of suffering, i.e., not just suffering for suffering's sake, but suffering with a purpose, and hence, dignity. Once we allow Jesus into the crosses of our lives, he can transform and purify them. He will instill meaning and purpose into them. He offers us the singular grace to accompany him in his own unique passion, that inestimable event of divine mercy. In the words of Faustina, through suffering, we are "assimilated" into Jesus (*Diary*, n. 604). What this makes rather clear is that suffering is not necessarily a denial of divine mercy. Mercy may well be, not only the means by which I can endure, but the placating end of suffering, its ultimate fruit.

Dark Nights' Revelation

As already mentioned, by nature, dark nights are steeped in divine mystery. So when coping with them, it's definitely advantageous to listen to those who already have personal knowledge of them. Based on their experience, God doesn't seem to alleviate the stripping pain, until we reconfigure the very "why" of our own existence according to gospel revelations and demands of holiness. God doesn't change heart, until we come to the willingness of soul divinely intended for us. In other words, we've got to change our heart. Dark nights and the consequent need to trust God's mercy put us mentally, psychologically, and spiritually in a stark, new, and challenging state of mind and soul. Dark nights can understandably repel, i.e., turn us off, or they can invite, impelling us to realign our life's guiding principle. They probe the subtle depths of our souls, which until now, we've kept protected from interference—including God's. There was no cogent pressure or reason to do so before. However, by God's sanctifying design, it's by acquiescing to God, surrendering to God that moves us beyond ourselves. Such relinquishing of ourselves to God's will and plan is pointedly the central reason for their presence now.

PARAMETERS OF DIVINE MERCY

Concurrent questions accompanying the seeming lack of God's affective and immediate mercy might well be: "What am I learning from this surface lack of God's mercy in my life? Where is God in all this? Why is God taking so long? What actually is God's will for me? Does God even want to help me?" As we've seen during the heavy pitches of a dark night, it is encouraging and hopeful to recall that not even the Beloved Son was sheltered from the Father's tough unbending plan. Neither was the Sorrowful Mother, neither were ions of struggling pilgrims on their way to holiness. It's also a bonus to realize that our own very limited notional preference of mercy comes in at a second place to God's plan. In other words, our notions and catechesis of mercy do not always fit God's. Again, "My thoughts are not your thoughts" (Is 55:8). Just because we sincerely love God doesn't mean that this same loving God is going to just cuddle us, certainly not try and test us. God wants our best! God knows plenty of things we don't and wants to see how far we can be stretched in the depths of our souls. The spiritual slogan: "Christ Wants More," is not about God exacting more for self but divinely scheming more expeditiously for us!

There's another image to help understand the transforming power of dark nights. Ever wonder how rich summer greenery turns into the stunning splendor of autumn colors? Depending upon the type of tree or shrubbery being considered, there are at least two different processes.

Most people have had the pleasure of seeing nature's yearly, autumn unveiling of surprise and color. We've probably all asked the question at one time or another: "How does that happen?" But you know what? Those compli-

CELEBRATING COMPASSION

menting colors of orange, red, and yellow have actually been there all the time quietly hidden behind a cloak of green chlorophyll. Then comes the question: "So how come we couldn't see them before?" Well, since it's the sun which generates the chlorophyll, it's understandable why trees are clothed in such a rich green pigment throughout the summer. But as summer begins to wane and as the day's light grows shorter and the trees spend more time in darkness, nature's mask of chlorophyll begins to fade. It's only then that the hidden impatient colors of autumn make their brilliant debut. In other words, rather than impeding a showy fall revelation, darkness is nature's strategy to reveal a tree's true colors.

Something similar occurs in our spiritual journey. The difficult times of life, the unforeseen crosses, the annoying pains, each and all constitute our dark nights. Some difficult times, some crosses, some pains we bring down upon ourselves. Some are imposed by others. But no matter their source, once God enters them, they become part of a divine strategy to bring about our soul's true character. Cultivated and nurtured by divine love, dark nights call forth a more vibrant Christlike character already present within us since the instant of conception.

There are other forests which do not have the rich stowaway of colors present in their leaves. So the color-producing dynamic is quite different. The autumn reds and purples begin developing in late summer, but this time, precisely due to the sun's bright light. The result of that brightness causes a so-called "breakdown" of sap sugars in the leaf. So it's just the opposite of the former group. In this class, when the days of autumn are bright and cool, and the

112

nights are chilly but not freezing, the most luminous colorations happily develop. In other words, what looks like a disheartening breakdown within the leaf, actually fosters a restless palette of unpredictable blush and beauty, and God is the artist.

Spirituality's Masquerade

In the spiritual life, while our testing might also masquerade as "breakdown," in reality, it is the concerted divine activity within. It's the persevering, shimmering light of Christ effecting our conversion. Rather than a breakdown, it's a humbling, ready surrender to that love-light of Christ, ushering in God's compassionate plan of intimacy. We experience the transformational impetus of "very truly, I tell you, unless a grain of wheat fall into the earth and dies, it remains a single grain, but if it dies, it bears much fruit" (Jn 12:24). It echoes: "I must decrease so Christ can increase" (Jn 3:30). Again, our true colors rise to the surface of our soul and character.

Forgiving mercy—whether it is of the rendering or the needing—can most often have a dark night shadow to it. As such, it also has a potential holy night glow to it. But often, it has to be patiently searched out before it can be embraced.

We often miss out on the joyful willingness of divine mercy. The stirring mix of true mercy fosters ready celebration. Again, recall the festive choices of a very pleased, exceedingly happy *abba* of the prodigal son. Could the prodigal son's mother have been any less pleased and jubilant? Hinting at an identical experience, scripture reminds

CELEBRATING COMPASSION

us, "There is joy in the presence of the angels of God over one sinner who repents" (Lk 15:10). When the Church refers to sacramental reconciliation, it has with reason traditionally been called a "Celebration of Reconciliation." Recently it's also been referred to as a "Festival of Mercy." Even the title of the special year set aside for mercy was referred to as a "Jubilee" year. A genuine exercise of compassion ought naturally to occasion meaningful relief and joy within both the forgiven, as well as the forgiver.

Absolutely not to be forgotten, an integral parameter—as well as critical, *sine qua non* condition, i.e., *without this you won't get that*—of receiving God's mercy, is being merciful with others.

> Eternal God, in whom mercy is endless, and the treasury of compassion inexhaustible, look kindly upon us, and increase Your mercy in us, that in difficult moments we might not despair, nor become despondent, but with great confidence submit ourselves to Your holy will, which is Love and Mercy itself. (*Diary*, n. 950)
>
> Happy are those to whom the Lord imputes no iniquity and in whose spirit there is no deceit. (Ps 32.2)

Either we trust in God's "holy will, which is love and mercy itself," or we don't. But what possible reason would Divine Mercy have to deceive us?

8

Sacraments of Mercy

For Christians, the word *sacrament* refers to seven special events inspired by Jesus to share divine life with us. Each one conveys God's presence in a reaching out to us. But that divine presence is not broadcast through a bolt of lightning, raucous thunder, or an angelic messenger. Rather we have a God who communes through ordinary, humanly visible "signs." In other words, God blesses and moves us through actions we can see and experience, e.g., a gentle human touch, an audible word, a visible gesture, and a familiar taste. By definition, signs point to realities beyond themselves. In this sacred scenario, these signs point to a loving God, caring for, and nurturing us. While all seven sacraments are an unmerited partaking in God's intimacy, five of them focus more intently upon God's merciful remission of our human failures. We call those "sin."

Baptism's Compassion

The first "Sacrament of Initiation" is Baptism. It's called such for two reasons. First, it's the gate to all the other sacraments. Secondly, it's the indispensable door to eternal life. "Jesus answered, 'Very truly, I tell you, no one can enter the kingdom of God without being born of water and Spirit'" (Jn 3:5). It's also referred to as "the first and chief sacrament of forgiveness" (*Catechism*. n. 977) for two reasons: first, because of what the baptismal signs, i.e., the words, water, oils, and actions taken together symbolize; secondly, because the divine embrace of Baptism is all inclusive of any possible sin contaminating the human soul.

Following the sin of our first parents, a wounded God could have rightly chosen to consign the human race to hell. But inherent compassion cajoled God to offer a second-chance alternative. We human beings are not just pure spirits but flesh and blood. God knew well that having no measurable quantity in itself, the human spirit would be best reached through our bodies which can, in fact, measure. Hence, Jesus sponsored perceptible, audible sacramental signs created for our benefit. But at the same time, God wants signs from us. Baptism is our first sign of surrendering to the Spirit; the first sign we give to God of our own readiness to renounce Lucifer's "I will not serve" (Jer 2:20). It is an indispensable sign that we don't agree with our first parent's deluded disobedience. Surrendering to God's merciful plan, we are not only set free from the grasp of original sin, but in that same moment, God prom-

SACRAMENTS OF MERCY

ises every single sacramental grace, every divine assistance of fortitude and fidelity we will ever need to belong to a Savior. None of this is for one instant because God has to do so. Rather it is because mercy pleases God. God really enjoys being merciful.

Due to its scope and irreversible character, Baptism is a once-in-a-lifetime occasion. There is no need to repeat it. Its absolving of original sin has been accomplished once and for all. Once seared by divine love and life, the person has been certified, reserved, irrevocably consecrated to the sacred forever. "See what love the Father has given us, that we should be called children of God, and this is what we are" (1 Jn 3:1), all due to God's mercy.

But how do we deal with sin committed after Baptism? Concretizing his own proclamation, "What I want is mercy, not sacrifice. I did not come to call the virtuous, but sinners" (Mt 9.13), Jesus propagates four additional sacraments of mercy for absolving post-baptismal sin.

Eucharist's Reconciliation

The fact that the ordinary sacrament of forgiveness for most sin is that of the Holy Eucharist is not broadly appreciated. Even though it's quite clear from Church teaching, many faithful just don't realize it. That's unfortunate. Of course, nothing is automatic here. All forgiveness needs to be steeped in honest sorrow, as well as intention not to repeat it.

For instance, *the Catechism of the Catholic Church* plainly states that "Holy Communion separates us from

CELEBRATING COMPASSION

sin." Explaining that such is one of the particular fruits of Eucharistic reception, it continues:

> The body of Christ we receive in Holy Communion is 'given up for us' and the blood we drink 'shed for the forgiveness of sin.' For this reason the Eucharist cannot unite us to Christ without at the same time cleansing us from past sins and preserving us from future sins. (*Catechism*, n. 1393)

By way of further explanation the next paragraph continues:

> As bodily nourishment restores lost strength, so the Eucharist strengthens our charity, which tends to be weakened in daily life; and this living charity *wipes away venial sins*. By giving himself to us Christ revives our love and enables us to break our disordered attachments to creatures and root ourselves in him. (*Catechism*, n. 1394)

Still later:

> Communion with the Body and Blood of Christ increases the communicant's union with the Lord, forgives his/her sins,

SACRAMENTS OF MERCY

and preserves him/her from grave sins. (*Catechism*, n. 1416)

St. Maximus of Turin (380–465) encouraged:

> Let no one, conscious of his/her sinfulness, withdraw from our common celebration, nor let anyone be kept from our public prayer by the burden of his/her guilt. Sinner s/he may indeed be, but s/he must not despair of pardon on this day which is so highly privileged; for if a thief could receive the grace of paradise, how could a Christian be refused forgiveness?

Pope Francis affirms:

> This is how we recognize that the Eucharist is not a prize for the strong, but a source of strength for the weak, for sinners. It's forgiveness, it's the Viaticum that allows us to go forward and move along. (2015, Corpus Christi Mass)

Remember the moving biblical account in the book of Isaiah (6:1–8) about a King Uzziah dying and going to heaven. Right away, he sees "the Lord sitting on a throne" around which are top-ranked angels attending him. In the midst of rising incense, they are calling out one to another, "Holy, holy, holy is the LORD of hosts; the whole earth is full of his glory." Immediately, the king knows he's in trou-

CELEBRATING COMPASSION

ble. In such sacred splendor, he is stunned with his own unworthiness to be there. "Woe is me! I am lost, for I am a man of unclean lips, and I live among a people of unclean lips, yet my eyes have seen the King, the LORD of hosts!"

Surely at the Lord's bidding, one of the angels, holding in a pair of tongs a burning coal taken from the heavenly altar, flies over and touches only Uzziah's lips with it. But Uzziah is cleansed entirely from head to foot. The angel announces good news, "See now that this has touched your lips, your wickedness is removed, your sin purged."

If the mere touch of the lips by the coal could cleanse his entire person, what must be the sin-dispelling power of Eucharist! Eucharist is not a heavenly ember scorching our lips but the true body and blood of Jesus in a consummating, searing union with our total person. "Though your sins be like crimson, they shall be as white as snow' though they are crimson, they shall be like wool" (Is 1:18). Factually, we have "our robes washed clean in the blood of the lamb" (Rev. 7:14).

However, the Church is equally unambiguous that if we have sinned in a deadly way, then it is the "sacrament of reconciliation," which is the ordinary means of resolution. "The Eucharist is not ordered to the forgiveness of mortal sins—that is proper to the sacrament of reconciliation" (*Catechism*, n. 1395). "Anyone who desires to receive Christ in Eucharist Communion must be in the state of grace," i.e., free of any deadly sin, i.e., any deep-seated disorientation from God. "Anyone aware of having sinned mortally must not receive communion without having received absolution in the sacrament of penance" (*Catechism*, n. 1415). But there is hope. "By the same charity that it enkindles

SACRAMENTS OF MERCY

in us, the Eucharist *preserves us from future mortal sins.* The more we share the life of Christ and progress in his friendship, the more difficult it is to break away from him by mortal sin" (*Catechism*, n. 1395).

There are various reasons why a person may opt not to receive Holy Communion. We would be a bit presumptuous, if not arrogant, to immediately judge s/he is in major sin. For instance, the reason may simply be they've not fasted for the entire hour before Communion time. Perhaps they have an upset stomach. Maybe they've already received Communion at another Mass. Still, it's true. Some people are caught up in some unplanned, moral web of life but still give themselves to the spiritual journey as best they can, such as physically participating at Mass. It's a meaningful indication of their lingering, if not, indeed, struggling love for God. However, though on the journey, there is still a need to resolve whatever morally hinders full sacramental reception of Eucharist. God surely doesn't miss their presence, which ultimately is a witness to Eucharistic significance. It's just such growing Eucharistic love which has powerfully changed lives from sinner to saint.

The Eucharist is, by God's plan and design, a preeminent sacrament of forgiving mercy.

Sacramental Reconciliation

Jesus, *the* living sacrament of God's forgiveness and mercy, begins his own public ministry with a beckoning call to exoneration and reconciliation. "Repent," i.e., conduct yourself in such a way as to be able to receive my mercy "and believe in the Good News" (Mk 1:15). The

CELEBRATING COMPASSION

Good News is that there's even a possibility of being forgiven for purposeful sin; that we even have such a God
willing to extend a compassionate heart and hand; that we
are offered a second chance.

The gospels are filled with accounts of Jesus' encoun-
ters with sinners, each and every meeting illustrating his
limitless compassion. To those who, in fact, showed sorrow
for their sinfulness, Jesus explicitly evidenced, equally by
word and action, their prompt pardon. There is the cure of
the paralytic (Lk 5:18–26); the sinful woman who anointed
his feet (Lk 7:36–50). He visited and ate with sinners, not
only out of a sense of dedication to ministry because he
was sent "to the lost sheep" of Israel (Mt 7:24), but more
importantly, simply because he loved them exceptionally
and with obvious fervor. He repeated parables about his
own Heavenly Father's constant and consistent love for
those who had wandered, i.e., those "lost sheep, the lost
drachma," the confused, lost "prodigal son" (Lk 15). He
taught "love of enemies" (Mt 5:43–48), the forgiveness of
another's offense "not seven but seventy times seven times"
(Mt 18:22).

Under the most unimaginable and personally stress-
ful circumstances, Jesus practiced and witnessed exactly to
what he himself preached, "Father, forgive them for they
know not what they are doing" (Lk 23:34), which in some
sure and certain way points to each of us who have a personal claim and involvement in sin. To live with this divine
life and love within us, to be one with Jesus' perfect love
for the Father is to be joined to his complete victory over
sin and its consequences, thereby, conquering death. It is

122

to share in the "crushing of the serpent's head" prophesized in Genesis 3:15.

Reconciliation: All Jesus' Idea

Sacramental reconciliation was all Jesus' idea. It began right after his resurrection. Jesus appears to his fearful apostles gathered in an upper room. Except for John, they had all been rather gutless in the past few days. Jesus could well have come bitterly complaining at irredeemable odds with them. But he comes not just to prove he is alive again, but he's going to send those apostles on a sensitive mission. Always the teacher and exemplar, Jesus sets the tone for that mission: "Peace be with you" (Lk 24:36). Jesus evidences only enduring love and acceptance, unconditional kindheartedness. It is an astounding event of unfathomable reconciliation. He's about to send those very apostles on an identical journey of unconditional compassion. "As the Father has sent me, so I send you... Receive the Holy Spirit. If you forgive the sins of any, they are forgiven them; if you retain the sins of any, they are retained" (Jn 20:21–23). "As the Father has sent me," the apostles and all their ordained successors would likewise stand in the very mission, Person and Spirit of God's "beloved Son," a mission, a Person and Spirit of complete, unconditional, joyful reconciling. With some accommodation, there echoes parts of Psalm 41:

> The Lord is kind and merciful, pardoning all our iniquities, healing all our ills, redeeming our life from destruction, crowning us with kindness and compas-

CELEBRATING COMPASSION

sion. Merciful and gracious is the Lord, slow to anger and abounding in kindness. Not according to our sins does he deal with us, nor requite us according to our crimes. As far as the east is from the west, so far has he put our transgression from us. As a father or mother has compassion on their children, so does the Lord have compassion on all who are soulfully concerned for him.

The sacred thread of love and compassion which runs through Old Testament prophets and then through THE prophet, the Christ of the New Testament, continues to prophetically resound in words of Pope Francis:

Among the Sacraments, certainly that of reconciliation renders present with special efficacy the merciful face of God. It concretizes and manifests it continually without stopping. Let us never forget, be it as penitents or as confessors: there is no sin that God cannot forgive! None! (March 12, 2015, to priests participating in a *Course on the Internal Forum*)

Simply put, penance and our dire need for divine mercy, hopefully resulting in concrete reconciliation, all exist pointedly because actual and personal sin is a reality. Though that reality of sin is universal, the sense of actual personal sin isn't always owned by individuals. How curi-

SACRAMENTS OF MERCY

ous because we are all sinners—the Lord has told us so. "If there is one among you who has not sinned, let him/her cast the first stone" (Jn 8:7). The Evangelist John doubles down: "To say that we have never sinned is to call God a liar" (1 Jn 1:10). There's the insightful spiritual awareness that says: "Ourselves we cannot save." Hence, we are in absolute need of a savior, a deliverer, who, in the words again of St. John: "appeared in order to abolish sin" (1 Jn 3:5), hence, to decimate evil actions. In the words of St. Matthew, he is named '*Jesus*' precisely because it is he "who is to save his people form their sins" (Mt 1:21), emphasizing the merciful recuperating of any repentant, wayfaring person. In other words, God's mercy is not merely aimed at alleviation of sin, but even more intentionally, is directed at an honest, seriously-striving pilgrim's holiness and consequent eternal happiness.

As only this "Son of God" could want to do, Jesus assumes to himself the panorama of all sin and its consequences in its totality. He's not called "Savior" for nothing. He reaches out in the sympathetic tone of the concerned Good Samaritan lifting up a wounded person from the ditch (Lk 10:33–37). He compassionately embraces any frightened sinner.

> Though your sinful actions be as striking as scarlet, I'll bleach them white, make them undetectable, hide them in the scarlet of my own blood. I'll take your place before my Father. And I will love you as truly as though your sins never occurred in the first place. I will love you back into

innocence. My forgiveness and compassion are absolutely complete and perfect.

The consoling truth about this Sacrament of Reconciliation is, in the act of being absolved of one's sins, Jesus is as truly present as he is in the Sacrament of the Eucharist. His intimate embrace is warm and sure.

However, while God's love is unconditional, God's forgiveness isn't. In other words, it demands first our own conscious contrition and purpose of amendment. "From now on, do not sin again" (Jn 5:14, 8:11). What the sympathizing Lord offers a repentant sinner is exactly what s/he (the sinner) longs for above all, namely hope! The Sacrament of Reconciliation is, indeed, a sacrament of merciful hope and second chances, being reborn to the innocence of our baptism.

Anointing's Reconciliation

There are two interlacing scriptural foundations for the "Sacrament of Anointing the Sick," treating of merciful healing in both body and soul.

> So they set off to preach repentance; and they cast out many devils, and anointed many sick people with oil and cured them. (Mk 6:13)
>
> Lord God, you have said to us through your apostle James: Are there people sick among you? Let them send for the elders of the Church, and let the priests pray

SACRAMENTS OF MERCY

over them anointing them with oil in the name of the Lord. The prayer of faith will save the sick persons, and the Lord will raise them up. If they have committed any sins, their sins will be forgiven them. (Jas 5:13–15)

The rather general insistence of Jesus: "Heal the sick" (Mt 10:8) is surely apropos here. From Jesus' own example, he often accompanied his healing of body ministry with words reconciling the soul: "Your sins are forgiven" (Mt 9:2, Mk 2:5.9, Lk,5:20).

Many people never have an opportunity to participate in the celebration of the Anointing of the Sick. Like the other sacraments, there is an unfolding ritual in preparation for the actual anointing. Beginning with a sign of the cross and a proclamation of the Lord's peace and presence, there follows immediately a sprinkling of all present with blessed water. That blessed water is a distinct reminder of one's own baptism. Then there's a pertinent scripture reading and an opening prayer leading into a call for God's forgiving mercy. It could be a shared expression of sorrow, or responding to the infirm person's request, the one-on-one celebration of the Sacrament of Reconciliation. There is a clear recognition here—physical ailment is quite different from spiritual ailment. Each has its own salve. This is not to say the spiritual cannot affect the physical nor vice versa.

Then, since Jesus so often physically touched the person he was healing, very appropriately there takes place a silent "laying on of hands" by the priest minister, i.e., "an

127

CELEBRATING COMPASSION

epiclesis proper to the sacrament" (*Catechism*, n. 1519). It's a calling down of the Holy Spirit. Fittingly then by invitation, family and friends of the sick person are also invited to lay hands on the sick person as an outward expression of their own love, healing petitions, and accompanying presence. Next comes the actual anointing the sick person(s).

Anointing the forehead with "the oil of the sick" in the sign of the cross, the priest prays: "Through this holy anointing may the Lord in his love and mercy help you with the grace of the Holy Spirit." The response: "Amen," i.e., "let it be so." Anointing the inside of the sick person's hands, again in the sign of the cross: "And may he who sets you free from sin save you and raise you up. Amen."

In reflecting upon the sacramental effects of this anointing of the sick and taking into account the very words of celebration, we discover a perfect match with the effects of Eucharist. In other words, there is an equal decimating of sin due to the commanding, purifying presence of God.

> This reality is in fact the grace of the Holy Spirit whose anointing takes away sins, and the remnants of sin, if any remain; this anointing also raises up and strengthens the soul of the sick person, arousing a great confidence in the divine mercy. (Paul VI, quoting the Council of Trent in his *Apostolic Constitution of Sacrament of the Anointing of the Sick*)

Said reality is truly a pleasant foreshadowing of the identical, fiery, purifying presence of the Holy Spirit awaiting our

SACRAMENTS OF MERCY

presence in purgatory. How consoling can it get? There's no doubt that, in serious sickness or at the potential nearness of death, Satan tries to get in his last licks. Additionally, there may be the fading of senses for the sick person, as well as possible worries about past waywardness of life. Comes the Lord in this sacrament of mercy, saying: "I myself will attend you—I myself will be with you. Do not fear. Trust my love, trust my compassion."

Thankfully, as different from years ago, when the anointing was mistakenly delayed as a last resort—meaning death seemed right around the corner—contemporary celebration is not "a sacrament for those only at the point of death" (Vat. II). It's for the "seriously ill." Paul VI reminded us that being "seriously ill" is a very relative term. The important thing is to call and inform the priest. Like Jesus himself, any minister ought to be lavish with the gifts of God without the least scruple. Beyond that and just to be on the safe side, it is impossible to overestimate the calming consolation of this merciful, personal, sacramental presence of Jesus if someone is actually at the threshold of death.

Following the anointing, there is an optional selection of prayers depending upon the reality. There are, for instance, two general prayers asking God to "grant comfort in suffering, heal his/her sickness and forgive sins." Another addresses "extreme or terminal illness," i.e., "since you have given him/her a share in your own passion, help him/her to find hope in suffering." Another takes into account "advanced age," i.e., where the individual is "growing weak under the burden of years;" another "before surgery," asking "the God of compassion" for healing presence.

CELEBRATING COMPASSION

There's one "for a child" beseeching God's "caress…shelter…tender care;" and finally, for a young person "in this time of sickness…restore [him/her] to health, strength… joyful spirit, ready to embrace your will." What a solacing, strengthening occasion of divine mercy and comfort for all partaking in this sacrament!

Following the anointing, if the sick person is actually in danger of death yet still able to receive Holy Communion, the Eucharist is referred to as "viaticum." Coming from two Latins words: *via,* meaning "way;" and *cum,* meaning "with," signifies "with you on your way." Talk about a merciful Christ personally accompanying us on our journey to the Father! But it's so much more than just taking us by the hand. Rather Jesus actually becomes one with our souls for the passage across to judgment and eternal life. What a God we have!

Then as compliment to the Sacrament of Anointing and viaticum, never as substitute for, there is the additional Divine Mercy encouragement:

> At the hour of their death, I defend as My own glory every soul that will say this chaplet; or when others say it for a dying person, the pardon is the same. When this chaplet is said by the bedside of a dying person, God's anger is placated, unfathomable mercy envelops the soul and the very depths of My tender mercy are moved for the sake of the sorrowful passion of my Son. (*Diary,* n. 811)

SACRAMENTS OF MERCY

Equally solacing is:

> Come to me, all you who are weary and
> burdened, and I will give you rest. Take
> my yoke upon you and learn from me,
> for I am gentle and humble in heart, and
> you will find rest for your souls. For my
> yoke is easy and my burden is light. (Mt
> 11:28–30)

Holy Orders and Mercy

The words of Jesus at the Last Supper, "Do this in memory of me" (Lk 22:19), can well be extended to all these sacraments of mercy. Establishing a new covenant priesthood
to be his loving presence in all sacramental actions, Jesus
assures all peoples of all times of his merciful, compassionate graces. Christ's own priesthood, passed on through the
sacrament of Holy Orders, is innately in-fleshed in his own
merciful heart. So when the Lord says, "Do this in memory
of me," he's commissioning his priests:

> Baptize not only in my name, but in my
> person. When absolving, be the occur-
> rence of my own welcoming presence to
> the suffering, humble repentant looking
> for hope and rebirth. At the moment
> of consecration during Mass, stand in
> my own priestly person—as I stand in
> yours—to make my saving Presence a
> reality in my own Eucharistic flesh and

131

CELEBRATING COMPASSION

blood. And in the unknown of sickness and/or approaching death, be my grounding, soothing presence.

Sacraments of mercy all.

This final reflection has been all about God's sacramental drama of mercy toward us. Praise God! But what about our mercy toward others? God anoints us personally to be contemporary occurrences of forgiving mercy. "For it is giving, that we receive" (St. Francis). It's only when we choose to be compassionate toward others—be they family, e.g., spouse, children, parents; be they friends, foes, fellow workers, or neighbors; be they government, church, priests, or pope—will we know the inner, distinct joys of "celebrating compassion." That's actually a real taste of God!

9

Mercy's Summation

Most people find forgiving difficult, but especially when matters are judged serious. However, opening our minds and hearts in prayer to the mind and heart of Jesus—even though reluctantly at the beginning—is a proven time-tested support and remedy. But if we really want results, then we have to pray with truly open vulnerable hearts. In other words, it's only when we have honest openness to interior change of our own heart that every word, every petition takes on a more purifying message. After all, why pray at all if in the end, we aren't willing to let God's presence, grace, and blessings actually change us? Why pray at all if deep down, we aren't willing to genuinely surrender our wounds? Why pray at all if we aren't hopeful of eventually releasing the person(s) who have offended us? This will be especially so when we pray and reflect upon the welcoming message of Divine Mercy.

Neither should we be afraid to compose or to adapt some prayer to fit our spiritual needs of the journey as we move through a forgiving process. In doing so, let's

CELEBRATING COMPASSION

remember two important truths: first, *celebrating compassion* becomes an indispensable, liberating way of life; second, Jesus' own words of condition, "But if you do not forgive others, neither will your Father forgive your trespasses" (Mt 6:15). Like that determined captain of the ship headed straight to a lighthouse we read about earlier, it's our, yours, and my call!

So here's an example of a creative prayer to be or at least to become always a thankful, humble forgiver.

Why not compose your own?

Loving Lord,
teach me why and how to be a Forgiver.
When faced with other's bitterness,
let me return only disarming love.
Help me to remember,
it's impossible to be gifted with peace,
without being a Peace-Giver.
When others are staggering beneath their woundedness,
give me the keen heart of a Samaritan Healer.
When others are despondent,
show me how to be a dispelling Guide.
Rather than measuring other's love for me,
may I be a ready compassionate Lover.
May I never forget,
to be filled with Eternal Life
I have first to empty myself of Self.
Instead of waiting for others to say,
"I'm sorry,"
may I be always ready to pardon,
since as a Forgiver,
I'm not only Christlike,
I'm the First to be set free.

CPSIA information can be obtained
at www.ICGtesting.com
Printed in the USA
JSHW020934241219
3173JS00001B/51